The Practitioner's Bookshelf

Hands-On Literacy Books for
Classroom Teachers and Administrators

Dorothy S. Strickland
FOUNDING EDITOR, LANGUAGE AND LITERACY SERIES

Celia Genishi and Donna E. Alvermann
LANGUAGE AND LITERACY SERIES EDITORS*

* For a list of current titles in the Language and Literacy Series, see *www.tcpress.com*

The Reading Turn-Around

A Five-Part Framework
for Differentiated Instruction

STEPHANIE JONES
LANE W. CLARKE
GRACE ENRIQUEZ

Foreword by Ellin Oliver Keene

Teachers College, Columbia University
New York and London

Published by Teachers College Press, 1234 Amsterdam Avenue, New York, NY 10027

Library of Congress Cataloging-in-Publication Data

Jones, Stephanie.
    The reading turn-around : a five-part framework for differentiated instruction / Stephanie Jones, Lane W. Clarke, and Grace Enriquez.
       p. cm.
    Includes bibliographical references and index.
    ISBN 978-0-8077-5025-4 (pbk. : alk. paper)
       1. Reading. 2. Individualized reading instruction. 3. Reading—Remedial teaching. I. Clarke, Lane W. II. Enriquez, Grace. III. Title.
    LB1573.J586   2010
    372.41′7—dc22   2009027086

ISBN 978-0-8077-5025-4 (paper)

Printed on acid-free paper
Manufactured in the United States of America

17 16 15 14   8 7 6 5 4 3

We dedicate this book to
all the children, teachers, and families
who defy labels every day.

Contents

PART II. CODE-BREAKING

PART III. MEANING-MAKING

PART V. TEXT ANALYZING

Foreword

Thank goodness for books like this! Stephanie Jones, Lane Clarke, and Grace Enriquez have created a masterwork that is simultaneously practical and groundbreaking. I have read few books recently that combine important reading theory with very useful, classroom-ready responses to the wide range of need we observe in children.

The model these authors use to familiarize teachers with the essential elements of reading practice is clear and beautifully illustrated with stories of children you'll swear you know. They highlight some of the most common obstacles that prevent children from living fully literate lives and provide useful tools and suggestions that teachers can use immediately. Importantly, these tools will broaden teachers' repertoire for dealing with obstacles *in the classroom* rather than feeling the need to call on outside specialists to "solve the problem."

The book is clearly organized and teachers will find themselves reading straight through it, amassing ideas to more effectively differentiate instruction for all readers in their classrooms. I believe, however, that teachers will return to this volume when a specific need arises for a particular child. The authors make clear that all five elements in their framework are intricately connected and that readers use them simultaneously, but suggest "foregrounding" certain elements in times of need while others are temporarily "backgrounded." Teachers will find these suggestions immediately useful when responding to children in conferences, in small groups, and in whole-class instruction.

I also encourage readers of this book to find a colleague with whom to partner for the teacher exercises sprinkled throughout the chapters. I am certainly guilty, as I imagine many of us are, of reading without thoughtful attention to the processes I routinely use to read fluently—adjusting my pacing and strategies to the demands of the text and finding ways to effectively use what I've read in the world. In other words, we teachers take for granted what we do naturally and effectively, but in order to teach well we must slow down and pay attention to our processes if we are to articulate to children what readers do to solve problems and engage deeply in understanding and acting upon what they've read.

The truly groundbreaking part of this book is the authors' wise and often startling evidence that we who work most closely with children may well be guilty of limiting our students' growth and achievement. When we label students as "struggling"—a term the authors recommend we abolish altogether—we begin to perceive of and act differently toward those children, unwittingly condemning them to more of the same uninteresting and decontextualized instruction year after year. Instead of using this reductive language, the authors argue for a more "generative and expansive" language to define and describe students' strengths, interests, and motives. They suggest that by knowing our students well and by building upon their strengths and interests in the real world, we will be able to avoid unnecessary labeling, special education placements, and possibly a lifetime of shame related to students' "disabilities" as readers.

Jones, Clarke, and Enriquez's call for change in our discourse comes not a moment too soon. Given the policy environment in which most educators work, we may actually find ourselves increasing the frequency with which we label and shunt children off to receive various "interventions." The authors argue that, for many children, the best "intervention" is a teacher who is well-informed in reading theory (which this book provides), who possesses a deep knowledge of students' individual interests and strengths, and who has access to a wide range of texts that can challenge and stimulate each child.

The Reading Turn-Around asks us to rethink our perceptions about children and challenges us to abolish some of our long-held beliefs and knee-jerk reactions to which we resort when a child mystifies us. This is a cup-half-full book that asks us to acknowledge the challenges children face from an intellectually curious, open, and expansive point of view. Exploring our own perceptions this way is worthy work—it could well change children's intellectual lives.

—Ellin Oliver Keene, May, 2009

Acknowledgments

Dozens and dozens of people, from our own childhood teachers to contemporary literacy theorists, have influenced the writing of this book. However, a few special people impacted the production of this text and need mentioning. First, thank you to Celia Genishi and Donna Alvermann for extending the invitation to write this book, Meg Lemke for her editorial expertise, Susan Liddicoat for her careful editing, Allan Luke and Peter Freebody for their conception of the four resources model, Barbara Comber and Barbara Kamler for their conception of turn-around pedagogies, and Desiree Grigsby for the photos used on the cover and opening Chapters 1 and 2. Several classroom teachers in Georgia, Ohio, and Florida read early versions of this text, provided feedback, and in some cases even let us use photographs of their classrooms: Thank you to Brett Axe, Jessica Fowler, Andrea Neher, Terry Nestor, Tonia Paramore, Jen Thiel, and Lori Thomas. And thank you to many others we have learned from across the years, especially Patti Baron, Kristin Beers, Jennifer Holwadel, Kim Lehn, Ella Revely, Liz Sturges, Connie Weethee, and the teachers at Fairview German Language School in Cincinnati, Maple Dale Elementary School, Oglethorpe Avenue Elementary School, Oyler Elementary School, P.S. 29 and P.S. 152 in New York City, and hundreds of others along the way. And most important, we thank the many students we have taught in our own classrooms when we weren't always perceptive enough to turn around our pedagogies in a way that might have been best for them. They are still in our minds and hearts and have pushed us through the writing of this book so that other teachers might not miss what we have in the past.

Stephanie would like to thank Casey for his love and encouragement; Hayden for her enthusiasm and inspiration; her mother, grandmother, fathers, sister, and brother for unconditional love and support; and Kim and Pam, two therapists who have eased the pain of repetitive strain injuries affecting her hands and arms.

Lane would like to thank Brock and Quinn for their love and support during this time of both writing the book and welcoming Ambrose to their family.

Grace would like to thank her parents for their boundless love and support; Jan, Leah, and Christine for their encouragement and cheer; her nephew CJ for his purple crayon; Michael for his wit, humor, and unconditional love; and Stephanie and Lane for their inspiration and friendship.

Turning Around Our Pedagogies and Our Readers

Have you ever felt like you're on a speeding train that is heading in the wrong direction? What do you do? Jump off? Beg the conductor to stop and let you off? Rally other passengers to force the conductor to turn around? Get off at the next stop, grab a map, and carefully plot your next moves?

The "struggling reader" train has, we believe, been moving in the wrong direction for some time, and we hope this book will cause you to pause, reflect, and carefully plot your next moves for reading instruction. In this book we offer practical advice for classroom instruction, but we also try to persuade you not to label any reader as "struggling" and to rally your colleagues against using labels that do nothing but harm children. By *do nothing* we mean that simply referring to a reader as "struggling" does not offer teachers, literacy coaches, intervention specialists, reading teachers, students, or families any real notions of what the student's assets are and suggest the direction for instruction. And by *harm children* we mean that the label "struggling reader" becomes an identity that defines a student in many restrictive ways: what she is allowed to do during reading, how he is expected to perform in other content areas, and how teachers treat her. The label can also be used as a reason for why he becomes withdrawn, why she skips school, and how he feels about education and himself.

For too long teachers have been persuaded to think and talk about readers who are not performing up to grade-level standards as "struggling," "behind," "resistant," "learning disabled," and so on. Our language is robust in naming potential things wrong with students but not in thinking and talking about *who students are, what they do well*, and *how they can teach us to teach them better*. One goal of this book is to expand teachers' understandings of and vocabularies about students who are not yet deeply engaged as readers in the classroom. Essentially, we hope to support what Comber and Kamler (2005) call "turn-around pedagogies," where teachers learn from students and then plan instruction. Inverting conventional modes of reading instruction is an attempt to turn around the work of teachers and open up spaces for students to turn around their engagements with schooled reading. Students can't and won't do it alone . . . teachers must do the turning first. Teachers can do this when they decide to stop riding what we have called the "struggling reader" train and instead lay new tracks that carry themselves and their students in new directions.

We focus on three moves for turning around reading pedagogies to lead to *expansive*, rather than diminished, student and teacher learning:

1. Know the student well and work toward productive reading identities.
2. Grow reading materials, practices, and activities out of students' interests.
3. Recognize and create opportunities for engaging students with real-world issues important to them.

Underlying these three areas are assumptions that classrooms can be flexible spaces where students work on different things and teachers differentiate their instruction to ensure every student's growth. It is impossible to create conditions for expansive learning when every day students are forced to read the same chapter of the same novel at the same time and respond to questions in the same way. In a test-driven curriculum, teachers are expected to follow a prescriptive instructional model, but we know most teachers find cracks in the curriculum to meet the individual needs of their students. As teachers and teacher educators work together to change institutional structures that don't allow for flexibility in meeting students' needs, individual teachers will continue to create spaces in their classrooms where powerful, relevant, and differentiated reading practices happen every day.

In this book, our approach to reading instruction has teachers asking lots of questions of themselves and of their students, instead of positioning themselves as authorities who already know the answers. Though we value strong and significant instructional practices from years past, research and theory continue to offer important insights for teaching and learning now and in the future. Our suggestions for reading instruction are not meant to be a silver bullet for all that is complicated about engaging readers in the classroom, but rather a launchpad for innovative, moving, relevant, fun, serious, and meaningful reading pedagogies in your classroom. We believe that differentiating instruction for readers must be generative and expansive, not reductive and diminished in the way some one-size-fits-all reading curricula are sometimes constructed.

Differentiation will mean opening up new ways of engaging with reading in school with many types of texts, many kinds of practices with those texts, and a willingness to follow students' interests so that they can lead more powerful reading lives.

OVERVIEW OF THE BOOK:
FOUR RESOURCES AND A FIFTH DIMENSION

This book contains five parts organized around four families of resources that readers draw on (Freebody & Luke, 1990; Luke & Freebody, 1999). We also explore what we call the "fifth dimension"—identity. In each chapter, we provide classroom vignettes, teacher self-examination exercises, practical suggestions for assessment and instruction and for working with English Language Learners, as well as illustrations and forms for documentation.

Part I invites you into our discussion. Chapter 1 presents our *framework* for thinking through reading instruction, largely based on Luke and Freebody's four-resources model, but also including a "fifth dimension" that foregrounds identities of readers. In addition, this chapter introduces the use of a Powerful Reading Plan (PRP) for individualized reading goals, and we include examples of completed PRPs in subsequent chapters. Chapter 2 discusses *identity* and the critical work that must be done around issues of identity in the classroom, particularly with students who have not experienced success in their schooled reading experiences.

Part II explores how students engage with *code-breaking resources*. Specifically, Chapter 3 addresses how students decode words as they read. This chapter focuses on word study and word work. Chapter 4 deals with how students grow their fluency for oral reading.

Part III is dedicated to *meaning-making resources*. Students use a variety of practices as they create meaning with the texts they read. The chapters in this section focus specifically on the connection–disconnection continuum (Chapter 5) and on enhancing vocabularies (Chapter 6).

Part IV discusses what Luke and Freebody call *text-user resources*. Readers use texts for different purposes, and this part highlights the teaching of and learning from non-narrative informational texts (Chapter 7) and digital texts (Chapter 8).

Part V focuses on *critical text-analysis resources*. Each chapter highlights one aspect of text analysis: text deconstruction/reconstruction (Chapter 9) and reading for social justice (Chapter 10).

As three authors, we write as "we" in some parts of the book and in others from the perspective of "I." We also directly address you as the reader, although we recognize that *we* are with *you* in this quest to turn around pedagogies to better engage, inspire, and serve each student. Our collaboration around this book is both a compilation of our individual experiences (represented by some references to "I" throughout the book) and our journey together as we read, think, talk, and shift our own practices in teaching and writing about reading. The classroom vignettes, teachers, and students we present are compilations of our time as teachers, staff developers, researchers, and teacher educators. While these are based on actual experiences in our research, teaching, and professional development, the vignettes have been fictionalized to offer succinct portrayals of readers and classrooms we have observed across many contexts. All names and locations have been changed to protect the identities of real children and teachers with whom we have worked.

PLOTTING YOUR NEXT MOVES

As you read this book, think about the choices you have. Will you continue riding the train that has betrayed so many readers too often labeled as "struggling"? Or will you begin to see your students differently and talk with them in curious and nuanced ways that will turn around your pedagogies to reenchant and reengage readers in powerful practices? Hopefully, this book will help you see alternatives to the same tired approaches to interacting with students who are not yet engaged in the reading process. The turn-around is up to you, and reading this book can be your first step.

Part I

A FRAMEWORK FOR THINKING ABOUT READERS

A Five-Part Framework for Powerful Reading

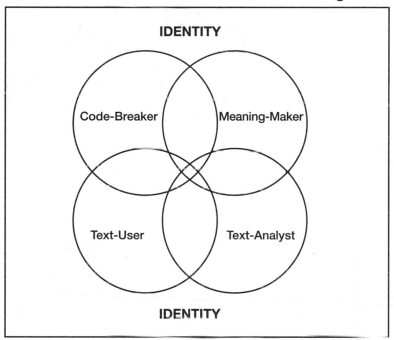

CHAPTER 1

Turning Around:
A Five-Part Framework
for Expansive and
Powerful Reading

Picture an enormous fifth-grade classroom where students are quietly reading a novel selected by their teacher. Following 20 minutes of sustained silent reading, the students gather in the front of the room to discuss some guiding questions about the chapter, except for two boys and one girl with their heads on their desks, sleeping.

W e are deeply concerned about these students' engagement with school and how sleeping through "reading"
class will impact educational opportunities. What is
more alarming is that the students have already checked out—they
have already decided that reading is not for them and too often believe that adults in their school don't care about them.

Many teachers find themselves in these situations every day,
with students checking out before there is an opportunity to help
them check in. The temptation is to say, "He's checked out—
nothing I can do." The more challenging response, and by far the
more ethical, responsive, and professional one, is to figure out why
the student has checked out and assume responsibility to check
him back in.

TURNING PEDAGOGIES AROUND

Barbara Comber, Barbara Kamler (Comber & Kamler, 2005; Kamler
& Comber, 2005), and others in Australia call the innovative strategies used to interrupt readers' trajectories of failure "turn-around
pedagogies." These scholars focus on turning around *teachers* and
pedagogies toward students, rather than on explicitly turning around
students and their presumed negativity and disengagement. Turn-
around pedagogies assume that every student in your classroom
is reading right now. Believe it or not, each student, even the three
who fell asleep during "reading" today, *is* reading. Some have read
that school and the reading activities you provide during class are
interesting and engaging. Others have read that school is not for
them and that the reading activities you provide for them during
class are horribly boring and disconnected from what really interests them. They are reading. They are reading you, they are reading
the social and political expectations in the classroom and school,
and they are reading the world around them. Your reading job,
then, is two-pronged:

1. "Read" students differently to better understand
   them.
2. Figure out how students' readings of the world can
   generate more powerful reading practices.

Here's one example:

Tyrrell was a fifth-grader who slept through most language arts instruction and occasionally became angry and aggressive for seemingly no apparent reason. His teacher insisted that urban kids like Tyrrell be exposed to whole-group novels (for noble reasons), so even when he and a few others demonstrated social, emotional, cognitive, and physical disengagement, she continued with whole-group lessons.

During this unit, the city where Tyrrell lived experienced civil unrest when an African American teenager was shot and killed by a White police officer. Tyrrell talked constantly about what he watched on television and saw outside his windows. With only a little nudging, Tyrrell's teacher began talking with him about his concerns and letting him read newspapers and search the Internet about the events in this city during language arts time. Following days of intense inquiry, Tyrrell invited some classmates to help him research police brutality in the United States—something that kept them impressively engaged for over a month.

Tyrrell was angry. He was angry that every day in class he had to read and discuss things that seemed to have no bearing on the real world around him. Even solid attempts by his teacher at making canonical literature relevant to him did not help. Yet when his teacher turned her pedagogy around to hear Tyrrell and support his desire to read and write about a personal, social, and political phenomenon in his world, he was strikingly enthusiastic, self-motivated, and academically successful.

We want to make three things very clear:

1. "Struggling" readers often seem behind their peers in certain literacy practices because they have become *disenchanted, disengaged,* and *disrespected* within their school literacy experiences.
2. Turning pedagogies around can reenchant, reengage, and rerespect students.
3. Turning reading pedagogies around means pushing against some conventional beliefs about reading interventions and making space for innovative literacy work that expands notions of texts and supports powerful reading practices in the classroom and beyond.

A FIVE-PART FRAMEWORK FOR
UNDERSTANDING AND TEACHING READING

As graduate students, we were introduced to a number of writers in education that we wish we had known in our early years of teaching elementary school. Paulo Freire, bell hooks, Mike Rose, and Lisa Delpit wrote books that we devoured. And there were others, writing specifically about issues in the teaching and learning of reading, who were tremendously influential in our thinking about literacy. We often wondered, and still do, why the publications of literacy researchers like Carolyn Baker, Barbara Comber, Carole Edelsky, Peter Freebody, James Gee, Yetta Goodman, Jerry Harste, Anne Haas Dyson, Deborah Hicks, Hilary Janks, Allan Luke, Brian Street, Pat Thompson, and so many others rarely cross the desks of teachers.

This book is infused with many of these voices because they, along with others, have informed our research and practice in the teaching and learning of reading and reading instruction. To make this book as reader-friendly as possible, we don't include many research citations, but we want to acknowledge the impact these individuals have had on us.

Drawing from research, we present five core findings in the teaching and learning of reading. We address each across the book, but we also integrate them as much as possible:

1. Readers' identities, or perceptions of themselves as readers and of how others view them as readers, need explicit attention in the classroom.
2. "Reading" print involves similar practices as "reading" the world as one interprets signs and symbols and makes meaning about people, events, and all experience. Drawing on these similarities is important for the teaching and learning of reading.
3. Reading is a social practice and therefore influences and is influenced by classroom dynamics. Explicit attention to issues of power and positioning in the classroom can enhance the reading classroom and powerfully alter readers' trajectories.
4. Readers engage more with school reading when they do so in meaningful, purposeful, and relevant ways. Therefore, creating learner-centered classrooms is imperative for constructing a powerful literacy space.

5. Readers draw on and use four families of resources as they expand and deepen their reading practices. The four resources include code-breaking, meaning-making, text-using, and text-analyzing.

These five core findings in the teaching and learning of reading are incorporated in our five-part framework for expansive, powerful reading. This framework incorporates the four-resources model (Freebody & Luke, 1990; Luke & Freebody, 1999) and a "fifth" dimension of readers' identities (see the Figure on the Part openers, pages 7, 29, 55, 79, and 107). Across the five parts of this recommended framework, we take great pains to consider meaningful, relevant, and learner-centered materials and pedagogy.

Four Families of Resources

Reading researchers and practitioners continue to ground their work in that of Luke and Freebody, signifying the importance of their assertions to both theory and practice. In constructing the model, Luke and Freebody argued that all readers need to be able to do specific things with print in today's society:

- Decode words by putting sounds, symbols, and meanings together *(to be a code-breaker)*
- Interpret meanings embedded in texts *(to be a text participant or meaning-maker)*
- Recognize and use various textual structures or genres to understand how a text works and how to use it *(to be a text-user)*
- Analyze and critique texts around issues of power, perspective, and social justice *(to be a text-analyst)*

Readers draw from many different practices embedded within each family of resources, meaning that there is not one way to break the code of print or analyze text. Additionally, because the four-resources model is nonhierarchical, all readers at all levels need to learn and use all four resources simultaneously in their reading. This alone is innovative, since many hierarchical models for teaching reading begin with sound/symbol relationships and move strategically toward "critical thinking" in reading. Though in Luke and Freebody's model one resource may be foregrounded at any time

TEACHER EXERCISE:
AN ANALYSIS OF YOUR READING

Locate a website on the Internet that you have not accessed before and begin to "read" it. Answer the following questions:

1. When you first access a website, how do you:

    Break the code of the text?
    Interpret meaning from the text?
    Use text features to better understand it (e.g., links, tool bars, images, video, etc.)?
    Analyze and critique the text?

2. When is breaking the code most important for you while reading a new website? When is interpreting meaning most important? How about using the text's features? And what about analysis and critique?
3. Does the importance of these four resources shift in your first reading? If so, what do you notice about how they shift? How might your answers be different when reading a memoir?

during a lesson, an individual conference, or a reading of a text, all readers need to build strong, expansive, and flexible repertoires across all four resources in order to be the kind of reader necessary in today's society.

Skills Versus Practices

Within each of the four resources categories, there are multiple "practices," with more practices being produced all the time by readers. Luke and Freebody have referred to their four-resources model as four families of *practices*, implying the intimately interconnected nature of the resources as well as the ease and flexibility with which readers should be able to engage all of them. Their use of "practices" instead of "skills" is worth noting, as it aligns with our assumptions about reading, readers, and reading instruction. The concept of reading "skills" is too often considered a static set of particular procedures one can easily learn from a teacher and apply to any text across contexts.

Just as you do not likely break the code of website text the same way you break the code of print inside a memoir, or interpret meaning from the website text as you do from a memoir, or critically analyze the two in the same way, you will not likely use a standard set of "skills" as you move between readings. Instead, you do different things with different texts at different times. The flexibility, agility, and different reading practices of avid adult readers indicate the broad, expansive practices students need to be immersed in to construct successful reading trajectories for themselves in school and beyond.

USING THE FIVE-PART FRAMEWORK FOR PLANNING INSTRUCTION

Instructional planning should grow from what you know about students and their reading practices, and while much "teaching" occurs spontaneously as you listen closely to a reader talk about her book, you also create instructional plans for explicit lessons in different situations. We include whole-group, small-group, and individual planning sheets to assist you as you plan for powerful reading practices in your classroom. We introduce these guides here and provide information in subsequent chapters to help you understand how to use them.

Whole-Group Recording Guide

A whole-class recording sheet helps you gauge the status of the class regarding each part of the five-part framework during your informal and formal reading conversations with students (see Figure 1.1). As you observe, listen, and interpret your students' reading work, briefly note how their practices relate to each part of the framework. We recommend dating your comments and using as many of these class records as necessary. If you see patterns across students, you can make decisions about whole-class lessons and small temporary groupings that make sense. This recording sheet could be used in conjunction with the small-group and individual planning guides to support differentiation and flexible grouping.

FIGURE 1.1. Whole-Class Recording Sheet

Class	Dates				
Student Name	*Code-Breaking*	*Meaning-Making*	*Text-Using*	*Text-Analyzing*	*Reader Identities*

Small-Group Planning Guide

Differentiation requires grouping students differently to focus on a particular practice. Sometimes you will have several students who are focusing on the same part of the five-part framework, and you can group them together for instructional purposes and peer support. A small-group planning guide can help you make decisions about small-group instruction (see Figure 1.2).

Powerful Reading Plan

In each subsequent chapter, we present a collaborative plan created by a student and a teacher. Although each plan focuses on one part of the framework at a time to align with the focus of each chapter, we reiterate that these individual plans for readers can (and should) include goals from more than one part of the framework. The student and teacher create the Powerful Reading Plan (PRP) together, with the student establishing a goal and plan for reaching this goal and the teacher committing instruction and support to the student in attaining this goal (see Figure 1.3). The plan's collaborative nature is essential to its success, as it creates conditions for both student and teacher to feel ownership and responsibility for reaching the goals. The plan includes a reflection section for both to complete once the goals have been achieved, encouraging each to articulate and explain the growth and change experienced. The PRP should be used as a driving force for whole-group lessons/activities, small-group instruction, and individual conferences with students.

We hope this book, along with the guides, will help you see readers such as Tyrell in a new way.

FIGURE 1.2. Small-Group Planning Guide

Target part of the five-part framework: _____

Date of initial grouping: _____

Students who will benefit from a focus on this part of the framework:

_____   _____

_____   _____

_____   _____

_____   _____

Instructional Plan
(record specific practices to be emphasized and materials used)

Whole Group	**Small Group**	**Individual**
_____	_____	_____
_____	_____	_____
_____	_____	_____
Materials Used:	*Materials Used:*	*Materials Used:*
_____	_____	_____
_____	_____	_____
_____	_____	_____
_____	_____	_____
_____	_____	_____

Reflection:

Next Steps:

FIGURE 1.3. Powerful Reading Plan

(completed by student and teacher)

Date of plan: _____

I, [name of student]_____, plan to grow my reading
practices, and over the next month I am going to focus on:

_____

_____

To reach this goal, I plan to:

1. _____

2. _____

3. _____

I, [name of teacher]_____, plan to help you grow your
reading practices, and over the next month I am going to focus on:

_____

_____

To help you reach this goal, I will:

1. _____

2. _____

3. _____

Date of reflection: _____

Student reflections on the goal(s) above:

Teacher reflections on the goal(s) above:

CHAPTER 2

Identity Matters

Otis Spofford was the book for me and even though I checked it out every two weeks for a year straight, I never read past the first chapter. I wasn't a reader and no one seemed to notice except the librarian, who was concerned about my one-book repertoire.

—Karen Spector

I magine one of your students in the same precarious position that Karen Spector (2009) writes about in the above quote. For some of you, this scenario may seem unlikely since you ask students to add their school library books to their independent reading collections for the week. For others, the scenario may seem improbable, as you have worked diligently to ensure each student's self-confidence and competence as a "reader." For others, you may have already thought of some students who might be in the book-checkout rut that Karen was in. And without a systematic way of integrating self-selected library books with the regular classroom reading instruction, you may not have noticed your students' patterns. All of us, however, recognize that Karen's practice was not productive, and perhaps you hope to be the teacher who would notice—and then do something to turn Karen's habits around.

WHAT IS A READING IDENTITY?

Karen's quotation points to something greater and more important than the details of lesson plans and reading instruction; it marks the significance of one's identity as a reader inside and beyond the classroom. Karen probably learned some important lessons across that year as her teacher "taught" reading, since most teachers are mandated to teach something called *reading* at one point or another during the day. But Karen didn't learn to *become* a reader in the school context, to live readerly practices, or to find reason and passion in reading. In the school library, Karen was performing as a nonreader; even an anti-reader, and perhaps a rebel against reading—showing that off with her habitual checking out of *Otis Spofford* (Cleary, 1953) for everyone—and no one—to see.

Becoming a reader involves much more than learning to decode and comprehend; rather, it means becoming a certain kind of *person*, a person who is a reader (and we often perform differently as readers in different contexts). There are different kinds of readers, of course: readers who can't get enough science fiction, readers who speak out against injustices in written texts, readers who compare newspapers' representation of stories, readers who devour particular authors' books, readers who spend hours with their video games, readers who talk with friends about their reading, readers who explore the Internet and learn unexpected things, and an infinite number of other kinds of readers. A reader won't likely "fit" into one category alone either; many readers read in wide, deep, and expansive ways across contexts and media, depending on the social and political situations in which we find ourselves. Karen, even if she received good grades in "Reading," had *not* become a reader beyond the practice of checking out and carrying around one book from the school library.

> **BY THE END OF THIS CHAPTER, YOU WILL:**
>
> - Understand the importance of tending to issues of identity in the reading classroom
> - Know specific practices for constructing positive reading identities for and with students in your classroom

KYLE: SEARCHING FOR A SPACE FOR HIS INTERESTS

Kyle, a quiet and thoughtful fifth-grade African American boy in an urban public school, drew in his writer's notebook every day. In fact, while the other 33 students in his classroom busily wrote *something* in their notebooks each day, Kyle drew page after page of humanlike figures in various poses and wearing various kinds of attire. He was a prolific artist, demonstrating so in his notebook without a single written word accompanying his drawings. His teacher, Ms. Knight, was frustrated with him and his lack of engagement in writing (which also crossed over to reading). She shared with me (Stephanie), a consultant in her school, that Kyle was "resistant" and probably trying to mask a "learning disability" by focusing on his artwork instead of writing because he also "struggled" in reading. Additionally, Ms. Knight considered reporting Kyle and his artwork to the principal because she perceived both as violent. Kyle was drawing semi-human, cartoonlike characters with swords, blood dripping from the occasional flesh wound, and often in sparringlike stances with fists clenched and feet kicking. In addition to Kyle's not writing a single word during the first month of school in writing workshop, he had drawn himself into a pathology. His identity was read by his teacher as struggling academically, resistant to reading and writing, potentially dangerous, and reason for official reporting.

GETTING TO KNOW STUDENTS WELL: WHO IS THIS READER?

Ms. Knight had had much training (both socially and through formal education) in recognizing, diagnosing, and remediating "problems" with students. She read a lack of engagement in school reading and writing as a coping strategy for a learning disability

> ## TEACHER EXERCISE:
> ## THINKING ABOUT YOUR STUDENTS' READING IDENTITIES
>
> 1. Without looking at a class list, write the names of each of your students, and indicate whether or not you think they have positive identities as readers in school or in other contexts.
> 2. Using the class list as a reference, note any students' names you did not write down on your own, and add those names. Ask yourself why you forgot them.
> 3. Complete the following statement next to each name: "_____ is the kind of reader who sometimes . . ."

yet to be diagnosed and remediated. To further complicate things, recent media attention to violence in schools had placed pressure on teachers to analyze student artwork and writing for any indication that a student might have psychopathic tendencies that could, hypothetically, result in violent behaviors. Ms. Knight, then, had been persistently positioned as someone who must be on the lookout for problems. When she told me about Kyle, I asked the first question that came to mind: "What does Kyle say about his drawings?" She looked at me quizzically and replied, "I don't know." I assured her that we couldn't know where to go from here until we understood what this artwork meant to him, and Ms. Knight agreed to have an open-ended conference with Kyle and bring what she learned back to me the following week.

The simple question "What does Kyle say about his drawings?" is intended to turn around a teacher's positioning, to encourage the teacher to go to students for information about what's going on in their schooling experiences rather than relying on outside forces to "frame" (Jones, 2006) and then label a student's performance in a classroom. Turning around a teacher's positioning toward becoming an inquirer of students can turn around classroom pedagogy, which can lead to turning around a student's trajectory as a reader in school headed in the wrong direction.

Conducting an Informal Interview with a Student

Like Ms. Knight, interviewing your students can help you get to know them and what you need to do in the classroom to meaningfully engage them. You can use the list of questions and prompts below in various settings and across time, but *always* ask them in ways that demonstrate your *genuine interest* and avoid making a student feel interrogated or accused of something. Ideally, this will lead to a real conversation, not simply a question-and-answer session. Be sure to suspend any past frustration, and be prepared to learn something new about the student, reading instruction, and perhaps yourself. If you get truncated responses, encourage the student to talk more by saying things like "Tell me more" or "Can you say more about that?"

1. Tell me about yourself.
2. What do you like to do when you're not at school?
3. What do you like to do when you are at school?
4. What do you wish was different about our classroom or school?
5. Talk to me about reading in books, online, in magazines, in text messages.
6. What does reading mean to you?
7. How could reading time in our classroom be better for you?
8. If you were the teacher, what would you do differently during reading time? During other times of the day when you read?
9. What is easy for you when you read?
10. What is hard for you when you read?

Analyzing the Interview

Once you have interviewed your student, use the framework in Figure 2.1 to think about how the responses can help you change your practices in the classroom.

WHAT TEACHERS CAN DO: TURN-AROUND STRATEGIES TO SUPPORT POSITIVE READING IDENTITIES

The following Wednesday, this same concerned, frustrated, well-intended teacher on the verge of reporting Kyle for violent tendencies and beginning a process to identify him as learning disabled entered her professional development group with a writer's notebook in hand. Smiling, Ms. Knight gave me the notebook and enthusiastically said, "He is totally into Anime. And when I told him I didn't know what that was, he couldn't believe it. He wrote a 14-page informational non-narrative text all about Anime."

This fifth-grade teacher experienced, in her own words, an epiphany during her conversation with Kyle: "I am making assumptions about students I don't really know." Turning her position around

FIGURE 2.1. Informal Interview Analysis

Use this matrix to record your student's interview responses that refer to issues of social dynamics, topics/lessons in reading, text availability, and the physical/mental work of reading

	Social Dynamics in the Classroom	Topics/Focus of Lessons in Reading	Text Availability (books, magazines, Internet, newspaper, etc.)	Physical and Mental Work of Reading (decoding, meaning-making, analysis, etc.)
Positive experiences noted in interview				
Neutral or negative experiences noted in interview				
Possible changes to make classroom reading meaningful and productive for this student				
Changes being made (include dates)				

TEACHER EXERCISE:
THINKING CRITICALLY ABOUT CLASSROOM PRACTICE:
HOW DO YOU ADDRESS READING IDENTITIES?

- Do I call attention to certain students as being "good" or "struggling" readers in one way or another? How does that impact all my students' reading identities?
- Do I make assumptions about what students are thinking rather than asking them?
- Do I know enough about my students to decide what additional reading materials and practices should be available in my classroom?
- Do I allow students to bring in texts from home for reading?
- Do I have a system in my classroom that allows for "reading" the Internet during independent reading?
- Am I aware of high-interest reading opportunities online that could promote reading practices and positive reading identities (e.g., online video games, fan sites for blogging, informational sites about high-interest topics, etc.)?

---

from problem-finder to that of inquirer, interviewer, and curious investigator changed Ms. Knight's perception of herself, her job, and her students.

Kyle's teacher learned that reading identities matter in the classroom. Tending to issues of identity can expand possibilities not only for a student you might be concerned about but for everyone in the classroom community as you learn more about one another and respect one another's interests, desires, and needs. We encourage you to do the following:

- Recognize students' reading practices as performances of identities that they may desire others to see in them.
- Work to reposition students who are on the margins of reading "success" as having exceptional gifts to offer others in the classroom.
- Encourage students to collect books, magazines, and names of websites they hope to read in the future.
- Decrease the focus on student "behavior" and concentrate on the strength of students' reading.

WORKING WITH ENGLISH LANGUAGE LEARNERS

- Encourage students to write, draw, and read about things important to them.
- Afford *many* opportunities for oral language communication (in any language) with peers during independent reading and across the day.
- Encourage positive reading identities in students' native languages.
- Pay attention to how ELLs are positioned in the classroom and actively reposition them as knowledgeable readers who are valued in the classroom.
- Explore interactive electronic books that can offer bilingual resources for pronunciations, definitions, and so on (e.g., Adobe Reader ebooks, www.bluejellyfish.com.au).
- Teach students to use online pronunciation resources to gain more confidence in reading English (e.g., www.howjsay.com).
- Introduce students to texts that explore the complexities of acquiring a new language in school (e.g., *I Hate English!*).

HOW THE TURN-AROUND IMPACTED KYLE

Kyle's participation in reading and writing in the classroom changed immediately following Ms. Knight's inquiry into his artwork and her subsequent changes in reading pedagogies. Together they prepared a Powerful Reading Plan (see Figure 2.2).

After Kyle wrote the 14-page informational non-narrative text about Anime, his engagement with writing continued as he constructed pieces related to Anime within different genres across time. He immersed himself in in-school reading and research on Anime both online and in the new materials on the subject added to the classroom library by himself, other students, and the teacher. His position as an "expert" on Anime in the classroom offered him some much-needed status to contradict his label as struggling or "not a good reader." According to Ms. Knight, Kyle "seemed" happier and participated more across other subject areas.

Two years later, Ms. Knight told me that this single experience had completely changed how she perceived students and her job. Everything changed at that generative, sustainable moment for both student and teacher: Kyle could reposition himself as a "reader" and a "writer" inside the classroom instead of the resistant,

FIGURE 2.2. Powerful Reading Plan

(completed by student and teacher)

Date of plan: *October*

I, *Kyle*, plan to grow my reading practices, and over the next month I am going to focus on:

Reading more during independent reading.

To reach this goal, I plan to:

1. *Bring in some Anime books I have at home to read at school.*

2. *Look up and read animation websites on the Internet during independent reading.*

3. *Get ideas for writing during independent writing from the reading I do.*

I, *Ms. Knight*, plan to help you grow your reading practices, and over the next month I am going to focus on:

Helping you to read more during independent reading and enjoy doing it.

To help you reach this goal, I will:

1. *Find Anime and animation websites online that you might be interested in.*

2. *Help you to use the texts to get your own ideas for writing during independent writing.*

3. *Bring in newspaper articles and other texts about Anime and the differences between students' and teachers' perceptions of it to explore critical analyses in texts.*

Date of reflection: *November*

Student reflections on the goal(s) above: *I have found a ton of information about Anime and animation I never knew. I can see why some adults get worried about kids liking this stuff, but I also think they're only thinking of one perspective and they're not seeing how smart you have to be to create Anime and animation and to understand it all.*

Teacher reflections on the goal(s) above: *We have learned a lot from Kyle's inquiry into Anime and animation, and other students are starting to bring in their hobbies and interests, too. Critically analyzing one's favorite thing is not easy, but Kyle began to see that if he could learn to critique Anime texts, he could better understand the perspectives of critics and better create a persuasive response to those critics.*

potentially dangerous student. The teacher repositioned herself as the *learner* in the classroom—not as someone who always looks for problems and has the answers. Identity matters, and with the help of an insightful and willing teacher, Kyle could reconstruct his in-school identity as a nonreader into a reader who was engaged meaningfully in the classroom.

CONNECTIONS TO THE FIVE-PART FRAMEWORK

Identity issues are intimately tied to all parts of the framework, since being perceived as "good" or "not good" in any part of it begins to construct a school reading identity.

- *Text-analyzing*: Sometimes seemingly negative classroom behavior can be explicitly linked to text-analyst practices. Instead of punishing broad statements like "Reading is stupid," dig into them and ask students if they know how to use that same critique with texts they read. Being critical of texts is often a good motivator for reading, especially when students don't have access to texts they enjoy.
- *Text-using*: Highlight the student's strengths and celebrate them— especially with other students: "Kyle is a great user of the Internet; if you want to learn how to read and find things on the web, go to Kyle."

Part II

CODE-BREAKING

A Five-Part Framework for Powerful Reading

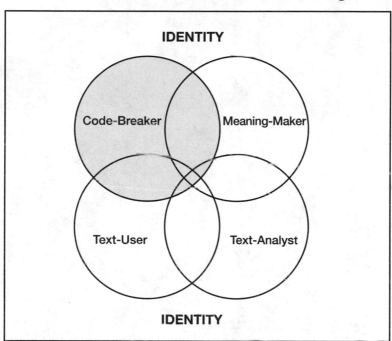

CHAPTER 3

Code-Breaking Practices

MICHELLE: OVERRELYING ON SOUNDING IT OUT

Michelle bent her head over the *Little Bear* book she was reading and stopped at the word *hope*. "/h/ /h/ /o-o-o/ /p/. Hop. I. Hop (short /o/). You. Like. It."

She looked at me (Stephanie) and pointed to the word *hope*. "Why is that e there?"

Michelle was in third grade at a school that, beginning in kindergarten, used an explicit phonics instruction program emphasizing phonics worksheets and phonics rules. By this time, she had been part of dozens of phonics lessons, several of them focusing on long and short vowel sounds,

---

BY THE END OF THIS CHAPTER, YOU WILL:

- Understand that decoding practices are integrated with meaning-making practices and extend beyond "sounding it out"
- Critically reflect on your teaching of decoding practices
- Have specific ideas for more expansive code-breaking practices

---

including the "magic *e*" rule reminding students that an *e* at the end of a word would usually make a previous vowel "say its own name." She had also completed numerous worksheets this year about the simple spelling pattern for *hope*, CVCe, because she was considered a struggling reader.

Later, while reading the story "Birthday Soup" in *Little Bear* (Minarik, 1978), Michelle used picture clues to decode *birthday* but stared at the word *soup* for several seconds before sounding it out: "/s/ /s/ /o/ /o/ /u/ /u/ /p/ /p/. s.o.u.p. [with short /o/ and /u/ sounds, making a two-syllable nonsense word]. That's not a word."

I sat quietly, looking at the text with her until she announced, "Soap. Soap. When two vowels go walking/The first one does the talking!"

Though Michelle had memorized most of the phonics rules she had been taught (except the "magic *e*"), they weren't helping her. Michelle sometimes attended to pictures for assistance in her problem solving, but she relied mostly on the *visual cue*, or the letters printed on the page, and her knowledge of letter/sound relationships for decoding.

WHAT IS CODE-BREAKING?

The written English language is a code of 26 symbols that produce many more sounds—or phonemes. For our purposes, the code-breaking practices of decoding and encoding are used to translate the code of the symbols into spoken language, and vice versa. Decoding is breaking the code of something that is already represented in symbols, or figuring out what something written down means, or "reading." Encoding is breaking the code of spoken language to figure out how to represent it in written symbols, or "writing."

Code-breaking is commonly linked to phonics and spelling, but it is intimately intertwined with meaning and syntax as well. To break the code of an unfamiliar word, a reader must quickly and flexibly move across three spheres of reasoning:

1. What does this word *look* like? (symbols/sounds)
2. What word would *make sense* here? (meaning)
3. What word would *sound right* here? (syntax)

These questions should be prioritized in the classroom through teacher demonstrations, student practice during reading, discussion about how students use them in reading, and visual reminders of the questions that students can easily access.

Many students who are not fully participating as readers in the classroom pronounce nonwords as they read and attempt to decode. And many of those students get more remedial phonics and phonemic awareness work. We argue that many of these readers are paying *too much attention to phonics* and not enough attention to *meaning*. Therefore, they should probably not receive more isolated instruction in phonics; instead, they need to recognize that the words they say as they "sound it out" *don't make sense.*

THINKING CRITICALLY ABOUT CLASSROOM PRACTICE: WHAT IS YOUR APPROACH TO DECODING?

How many times today have you said, "Sound it out"? How many times did you hear this phrase as a child from family members or your teachers at school? From colleagues at school today? You can use the following questions to examine your instruction in decoding:

- Do I say "Sound it out" to my students without being specific about what I want them to do?
- Do I encourage my students to be detectives who investigate the structures of spelling and pronunciation?
- Do I expect my students to use meaning ("Does that make sense?") and syntax ("Does that sound right?") to confirm or challenge their attempts to decode new words?
- Do I model all the ways an unfamiliar word can be decoded?
- Do students have access to a visual reference to prompt multiple ways of decoding an unfamiliar word?

- Do I individualize spelling lists that support particular readers' decoding practices?
- To teach phonics, do I use a prescribed curriculum or what I see my readers/writers using in the classroom?
- Do I teach phonics separate from reading and writing, or do I integrate them to be sure students can *use* their knowledge of letter/sound relationships?

GETTING TO KNOW STUDENTS WELL: WHAT ARE THEIR DECODING PRACTICES?

In addition to seeing Michelle as having trouble with reading, Michelle's teacher, Ms. Turner, also needed to recognize Michelle as a reader curious about spelling patterns. Her simple question "Why is that *e* there?" can prompt a spontaneous—but also long-term—inquiry into spelling that could be more meaningful to her than the current phonics lessons. You can ask yourself the following questions about your students' decoding practices to better plan their future reading instruction:

- Does this reader recognize when a word she reads doesn't make sense?
- Does this reader systematically move through the sounds in a word from left to right, or is she locating "chunks" of words for decoding?
- Does this reader know to skip an unknown word, read the rest of the sentence, and come back to try to decode it?
- Does this reader use the picture to help with decoding?
- Does this reader recognize words she has seen in other places? ("Oh, I read that word in the other book!")
- Does this reader use her fingers to cover up word parts (root words, affixes) to better decode?
- Does this reader decode easier once she has read a page, passage, or book quietly?
- Is this reader curious about word parts, spelling patterns, anomalies in spelling?
- Does this reader get nervous in oral reading performances, and does this lead to a perceived problem with decoding?
- How are this reader's encoding practices (spelling in writing) similar to or different from her decoding practices? How can they be used to scaffold each other?

WHAT TEACHERS CAN DO: TURN-AROUND STRATEGIES TO SUPPORT CODE-BREAKING

Many teachers use "sound it out" as a stand-in for a variety of decoding practices. But you can help students engage in more effective code-breaking by using more specific language prompts, such as the following:

1. Think about the initial sound and a word that makes sense and begins with the same sound.
2. Look at the picture for a clue about what the word might mean.
3. Skip the word temporarily, read to the end of the sentence, and then come back to see what word makes sense.
4. Find any chunks in the word that you already know, including root words, prefixes, and suffixes.
5. Think about a word you know that looks like this word.
6. Think about where you have seen this word before.
7. If it is a long word, look for syllables that might be broken apart.
8. Say the word aloud and read it in the sentence to see if it makes sense and sounds right.
9. Use all these practices *together* to figure out this unknown word.
10. If nothing else works, make a note on a Post-it so you can ask someone about it.

Encourage a Culture of Curiosity and Inquiry Around Spelling

Simple questions like "What do you notice about this word?" or "Where have you seen a spelling like this before?" encourage students to view words through a detective's eyes. Orthography, or "spelling," offers infinite opportunities for detective work. As a student begins to see himself as an orthography detective, his awareness around issues of spelling will grow as he reads and as he writes. He can reserve a special section of his reader's notebook for his orthographic discoveries, noting spelling patterns as well as unusual spellings of words that he discovers while reading.

Introduce and Study Onsets and Rimes

Rimes (not *rhymes*—though they *do* rhyme) are word parts comprised of a vowel and at least one consonant that make a distinct

FIGURE 3.1. High-Frequency Rimes

ack	ail	ain	ake	ale	ame	an
ank	ap	ash	at	ate	aw	ay
eat	ell	est	ice	ick	ide	ight
ill	in	ine	ing	ink	ip	it
ock	oke	op	ore	ot	uck	ug
ump	unk					

word chunk. Often called "word families" (Bear, Invernizzi, Templeton, & Johnston, 2008), these chunks are believed to be more helpful to readers than individual phonemes, or individual "sounds" of letters, which are often the focus of phonics worksheets. Thirty-seven rimes have been widely accepted as high-frequency word parts that can generate 500 early reading words (Strickland, 1998; Wylie & Durrell, 1970) and hundreds more when words become multisyllabic through the addition of prefixes and suffixes (see Figure 3.1). We recommend teaching one rime at a time, allowing students to play with the pattern, adding and subtracting multiple "onsets" (or beginning sounds) as well as exploring multiple prefixes and suffixes with generated words (see Figure 3.2). Small groups or whole classes can investigate rimes and display them on classroom charts, where readers and writers can easily access and refer to them. Additionally, some students may generate their own individual word lists for each rime in reading and writing folders for easy access during independent work time.

FIGURE 3.2. An Example of a Student and Teacher Collaborative Onset and Rime Activity for -*ate*

With a prefix	-*ate* words	With a suffix
	ate	
	Cate	
predate	date	dating; dated
	fate	fated; fateful
mitigate; irrigate	gate	gated; gating; irrigation
berate; irate	rate	rated; rater; rating
	late	latent; lateness

Demonstrate Specific Decoding Practices

Whole-class or small-group lessons can highlight multiple practices readers use for decoding (such as those listed earlier in this
chapter). We recommend that each lesson focus on one practice at
a time, with group or individual support for readers to practice the
approach in their reading.

Encourage Students to Write, Write, Write

When students have opportunities to write about things important to them, they work harder to break the code of the English
language. Communication becomes urgent when students' motiva-
tions are high for representing *something* to someone else for some
good reason through letters, petitions, memoirs, stories, poems,
blogs, instant messages, and so forth.

For readers who find decoding words in books difficult in the
classroom, writing their own texts (or *encoding*) for reading may be
an option that produces more success and therefore motivation for
reading/writing. Writers learn about the code of the English language from the inside out: They say a word aloud or in their minds,
and letter by letter they encode it to create its written representation
on a page or screen. The more fluent, flexible, and efficient *encoders*
students become as writers, the more fluent, flexible, and efficient
decoders they will become as readers.

Transcribe a Student's Composition

Some students find it frustrating to write a complex composition they have in their minds. Teachers can write or type a student's
oral composition about a topic that interests her that will then be
used as her reading material. Because the transcription is word for
word (resist the temptation to "correct" a student's word choice
if she is writing in English as her native language, but sensitively
help with word choice and sequence if she is writing in English as
a nonnative language), the student receives more support from the
text for decoding as she reads it.

Some researchers suggest that digital media stimulate rich and
complex language production for a composition (Labbo, Eakle, &
Montero, 2002). Video games, websites, videos, or photographs

may be used as a starting point for language production, written composition, decoding the writing, and reading.

Utilize Whole-to-Part-to-Whole

A whole-to-part-to-whole approach to phonics learning begins with a *whole* text such as a poem, instructions, a newspaper article, a letter, a story, and so on. The reading of the whole text focuses on just that: the entire meaningful experience of the text. Select a *part* of the text for productive code study, such as a high-frequency word, high-frequency rime, prefix, suffix, or consonant combination. After isolating the *part* for in-depth study, help the reader(s) focus on getting meaning from the text as a whole.

Begin with the Known

Using words that students are already familiar with—such as their first names, family names, names of products and places, high-frequency words, words from favorite books, and so on, to generate new words with similar sounds and patterns is always fun and motivating.

Expose Students to Rich and Varied Vocabulary

Using letter/sound knowledge to pronounce *disintegrate* will not help a student recognize it as a real word if he has never heard a word that sounds like it. However, he will be more likely to have heard a word similar to *disintegrate*—and therefore have an easier time decoding it—if he is immersed in a rich language environment at school. This doesn't mean, though, that he will necessarily understand what *disintegrate* means, so further attention to vocabulary (Chapter 6) beyond code-breaking is imperative.

Introduce Talking Dictionaries

Online talking dictionaries give pronunciations and sometimes definitions, synonyms, and antonyms as well. Looking up *integrate* on www.merriam-webster.com, one can hear its pronunciation, find its syllabication, read multiple definitions, and read about its etymology. Therefore, when a student comes across *disintegrate* in her reading, she will know that *dis-* is a prefix and can look up the rest of the word with which she is unfamiliar: *integrate*.

WORKING WITH ENGLISH LANGUAGE LEARNERS

A reader who is learning English must rely heavily on visual cues—his knowledge of letter/sound relationships or recognition of whole words—for decoding. A reader's developing English vocabulary may not help him in asking "Does that make sense?" Likewise, his growing knowledge of the structure of English probably won't help him answer "Does that sound right?" because nothing may sound right (or, on the contrary, everything might sound strange and therefore "right"). Teachers can help ELLs with decoding in the following ways:

- Encourage ELLs to talk with both native and nonnative speakers of English in order to stimulate oral English vocabulary and aid in the decoding process during reading.
- Engage students in small-group echo reading and choral reading of high-interest texts, and pull one or two spelling patterns from the text for generating new words (e.g., *-ight* and *-ay* from *A Day's Work* by Eve Bunting, 1994).
- Transcribe stories/instructions/poems for students in English, being careful to maintain the integrity and sophistication of the composition while also simplifying it to make it readable for them. Use these as classroom reading materials, and work with students to select one or two spelling patterns at a time to investigate and use for generating more words.

Encourage Students to Become Independent Code-Breakers

Individualized spelling dictionaries allow the student and/or teacher to accumulate correctly spelled words that are sometimes challenging for him, building the dictionary across time. The dictionary can be blank to begin with, or it can include some high-frequency words students might use regularly in their writing. Combining this with the "I'll tell you how to spell one word per day" rule during writing time will encourage students to be more active independent encoders while writing and help them to decode while reading.

Readers can also create bookmarks that remind them of everything they can do when they approach an unfamiliar word. These should be individualized for a reader but might include any of the practices listed earlier in the chapter.

HOW THE TURN-AROUND IMPACTED MICHELLE

The turn-around necessary to help Michelle use more powerful and expansive decoding practices included moving away from worksheets and individual phonics rules that weren't helping her during reading. Figure 3.3 shows the Powerful Reading Plan that Michelle and her teacher developed. Michelle was a good rule-follower, and once Ms. Turner demonstrated how readers can ask themselves "Does that make sense?" while reading, Michelle did this regularly. This often happened after she read a sentence, which prompted her to return to the new word and attempt to self-correct any miscues. The turn-around was a small one, but it helped Michelle tremendously as a code-breaker:

- She focused on meaning along with her letter/sound knowledge.
- She began recognizing rimes from other books and her own writing.
- She stopped saying each individual sound of an unknown word multiple times, began looking at chunks of words, and thought about meaning, too, thus improving her efficiency.
- She began thinking about word chunks in her writing instead of focusing on individual sounds.

Ms. Turner encouraged the entire class to be orthography detectives, which made classroom word work more interesting and motivating for everyone.

FIGURE 3.3. Powerful Reading Plan

(completed by student and teacher)

Date of plan: *November*

I, *Michelle*, plan to grow my reading practices, and over the next month I am going to focus on:

Using a lot of ways to figure out hard words.

To reach this goal, I plan to:

FIGURE 3.3. *continued*

1. *Make a bookmark of four things I can do when I try to figure out a new word (say the first sound, look at the picture, read the word, ask myself if it makes sense).*

2. *Always ask myself, "Does that make sense?" If it doesn't, an alarm should go off in my mind!*

3. *Start collecting words I notice that have the silent e at the end.*

4. *See if I can find patterns in my silent e words (like –ope words or –ate words that we worked on).*

I, *Ms. Turner*, plan to help you grow your reading practices, and over the next month I am going to focus on:

Using many ways to figure out new words as you read.

To help you reach this goal, I will:

1. *Help you focus more on "Does that word make sense?" when you are figuring out a new word in your reading.*

2. *Help you start a spelling dictionary to use during your writing.*

3. *Hold small groups during reading/writing time to look closely at onsets, rimes, and patterns readers and writers use to read and write words and make individual copies for you to keep in your folder.*

4. *Start an "Orthography Detectives" bulletin board so all students can begin to notice spelling patterns like you did when you asked, "Why is that e there?"*

Date of reflection: *December*

Student reflections on the goal(s) above: *Now I don't only think about the sounds in the words, I think about the pictures and what would make sense. It's been fun to notice all the silent e words and also to be a detective. I noticed a lot more about words in my reading and in my spelling, too.*

Teacher reflections on the goal(s) above: *Helping Michelle to be more curious about spelling patterns in her reading and writing has really helped me to be more curious about these as well. The whole class has really started to be "Orthography Detectives," and it has changed the way we talk about figuring out new words in reading and spelling unfamiliar words in writing. Michelle is routinely making sure her "guesses" at new words make sense, and I'd like to help her recognize more chunks of words as she decodes—this is something that she is still not doing regularly.*

CONNECTIONS TO THE FIVE-PART FRAMEWORK

- *Meaning-making*: Decoding and meaning-making should go hand in hand. Having individual word walls, being a word collector, and noticing words and word patterns help connect decoding with meaning-making.
- *Text-using*: Students should decode words from different types of texts. The teacher could model using decoding practices from a webpage or nonfiction book, teaching students to use different texts as they practice their code-breaking skills.
- *Text-analyzing*: Students will become better decoders if what they read inspires them. When reading "Birthday Soup," Michelle did not connect soup with birthdays, but if she was in the habit of questioning what was presented as "normal" in books, she might have found it interesting that soup was presented as a normal food in Marinik's planning of a birthday celebration. Paired with *Uncle Willie and the Soup Kitchen* (Disalvo-Ryan, 1997), "Birthday Soup" might inspire an inquiry into food, celebrations, and scarcity.

CHAPTER 4

Oral Reading Fluency Practices

CASSIDY: DEPENDING ON HELP FROM OTHERS

Cassidy was a small, African American third-grader attending a suburban school that was racially and economically diverse. She was quiet, always helpful to her classmates and teacher; she seldom raised her hand or spoke in class without being asked—the type of student who often falls through the cracks. One day Cassidy was reading aloud from the Junie B. Jones book that her small group was reading with their teacher. She tracked every word slowly, reading in starts and stops, word by word. When Cassidy paused, Ms. Matthews (Cassidy's teacher) intervened: "Get your mouth ready" and "Think about what would make sense" were two statements she said automatically with each pause. As Cassidy made the sound of the initial letter in the word, she looked at Ms. Matthews, who told her, "You have seen this word before." After 2 seconds passed, Ms. Matthews pointed to the word and carefully enunciated "weather." She then said, "Let's read it together." A similar scene played out during the next sentence when Cassidy paused at "tornado." Cassidy glanced up frequently from her reading, looking for affirmation or anticipating correction from her teacher or peers.

WHAT IS FLUENCY?

Fluency, as defined by the National Reading Panel's *Put Reading First* (Armbruster, Lehr, & Osborn, 2001), is the ability to read text accurately and quickly. In addition, students who are fluent readers adjust their pacing; stress appropriate syllables, words, and phrases; read with expression; and adjust intonation. Fluent oral reading is what captivates audiences, enables readers to personalize a text, and brings printed text to life. Furthermore, research has shown that as students' fluency improves, so do a host of other factors related to reading, including the tendency to read, reading comprehension, and self-esteem (Allington, 2005; Rasinski & Padak, 2000).

THINKING CRITICALLY ABOUT CLASSROOM PRACTICE: ARE YOU INTERRUPTING FLUENCY?

Before concluding that a student is a nonfluent reader, carefully consider your teaching practices when students are reading aloud. Teachers often intervene too quickly (interrupting attempts at fluency) when presumed "struggling" readers pause, stop, or begin to reread. Interestingly, many teachers wait longer before intervening

---

By the end of this chapter, you will:

- Understand why fluency is a code-breaking practice
- Be able to analyze your teaching, or verbal feedback, when a student reads aloud
- Have specific tools for getting to know your students better that you can use for fluency assessment and documentation
- Have specific suggestions for growing students' fluency practices

> ### TEACHER EXERCISE:
> ### THINKING ABOUT YOUR OWN FLUENCY PRACTICES
>
> - Find a text that you love to read. Read it aloud to a partner. Have the partner note what *you* do as a fluent reader to make the text "come alive."
> - Listen to a speech given by a famous orator—Martin Luther King Jr., Barack Obama, John F. Kennedy, Maya Angelou. What oral reading fluency practices do they use?
> - Do your findings align with the kinds of practices you encourage your students to use in oral reading?

when a presumably "successful" reader exhibits similar behavior. You might ask yourself: What came first, the nonfluent reading or the teacher's practice of interrupting? Try analyzing your practices with oral reading using the following questions:

- Do I give students ample time (3–5 seconds) before intervening with a prompt or the word?
- Do I interrupt, correct, or give clues to perceived "struggling" readers more often than to "good" readers?
- Am I correcting miscues even when they don't interfere with meaning? If so, why?
- What types of prompts for oral reading miscues do I provide and why?
- How do I handle interruptions from other students during oral reading?
- Does my intervention influence self-correction or dependence on others?
- What kind of feedback do I *not* give readers? Would they benefit from any of these?
- Does any of my feedback confuse readers?
- Does my feedback turn into spontaneous lessons when students miscue? If so, why? When are these useful and when are they distracting?
- Do I analyze miscues to better understand the strategies readers use?
- Does my feedback help students become independent, self-monitoring readers?

Despite teachers' good intentions, often their practices lead students to depend on someone's intervention when they encounter an unknown word. Ideally, you want your readers to do just the opposite: become more independent in their reading, including decoding unfamiliar words. When a teacher or peer jumps in with prompts or tells the word to the reader, why—and how—would a reader learn to employ decoding practices independently? Not only does persistent intervention in students' oral reading foster their development of dependent practices, it also begins to construct the student as a *particular kind of reader*—someone who *needs* intervention.

GETTING TO KNOW STUDENTS WELL: HOW DO YOU ASSESS A STUDENT'S FLUENCY?

To engage in pedagogies that interrupt trajectories of "failure" or "at-riskness," you need to *know your students well*. Instructional plans should be constructed with information gained from both informal and formal assessments. Simple, static labels such as "nonfluent" or "struggling" don't offer insight the way a more elaborated description of a student's oral reading might.

Using Qualitative Formative Assessment

A qualitative assessment uses a list of desirable oral reading characteristics as a formative tool to focus on what a student *does* during oral reading. Make a copy of the list shown in Figure 4.1 for each student, and use it as ongoing documentation of students' oral reading practices during informal and formal interactions. Additionally, the list can be used as a guide for whole-group, small-group, and individual lessons. When readers have been exposed to concrete examples of each characteristic, the list can be posted in the classroom, photocopied for students' reading notebooks or folders, or even copied on individual readers' bookmarks.

Using a 60-Second Assessment

A 60-second read-aloud can be used with students to document changes in speed across time and represent them on a line chart. To conduct a 60-second read-aloud, do the following:

Figure 4.1. Qualitative Fluency Assessment

A fluent reader: _____

(student's name)

___ Points to words for temporary tracking or to help decode a challenging word

___ Changes pace to align with the tone of the text

___ Reads in phrases

___ Rereads for phrasing or to adjust expression or intonation

___ Reads with expression and intonation, indicating attention to punctuation

___ Reads with expression and intonation indicating attention to meaning

___ Self-corrects miscues that interfere with meaning

___ Reads with appropriate volume and pace

___ Reads words automatically, with occasional pausing for explicit decoding work

1 = Almost all the time

2 = Some of the time

3 = Infrequently

Comments:

---

1. *Pull the student aside.* Nothing is more distracting or unfair to you and the reader than trying to listen to an oral reading while 13 other things are happening around you.
2. *Choose (or have the reader choose) an appropriate text in the student's independent reading range.* Remember that you are not out to "get" students by giving them a brand-new, tricky, or boring passage; rather, you are trying to learn about how they read aloud.
3. *Ask the student to first read the text quietly.* When students read the text once quietly before reading aloud for a fluency assessment, they benefit from a "warm" reading.
4. *Ask the student to read aloud for 60 seconds.* Remember to discretely keep track of time while simultaneously documenting:
   * *Accuracy checks*: Use tally marks to track words read correctly as well as miscues.
   * *Qualitative jots*: Jot notes about expression, intonation, pausing, phrasing, and so on.

5. *Graciously thank the student.* Framing the 60-second read-aloud as a collaborative endeavor between teacher and student repositions the student to be in control of her learning.

6. *Calculate words per minute.* There are certain benchmarks for the number of words per minute at various "levels" of reading (Harris & Sipay, 1990). To calculate words per minute:
   - Document the number of words read *accurately*.
   - Write the date and title of the text used on the bottom edge of a piece of graph paper to begin a line chart documenting words-per-minute reading across time.

Be careful not to overemphasize speed at the expense of emphasizing the broader context of *fluency*. However, for a reader such as Cassidy, whose speed is constantly interrupted by shifting eye contact and tenuous confidence, encouraging sustained attention to text and speed might be important goals.

How Often Should You Assess a Student's Fluency?

Since many teachers are inundated with formal, mandated assessments that can erode valuable instructional time, we recommend the following:

1. Periodic *informal* assessment of fluency is necessary for all readers. These assessments can include taking anecdotal notes during a conference as well as using the checklist provided in Figure 4.1 during small- or whole-group oral reading.

2. Additional and more frequent assessments of fluency are necessary for students who are not yet confident, fluent oral readers of texts familiar to them. Additional assessments, however, *should focus on the challenges of the individual reader* (e.g., phrasing, accuracy, pacing, self-correcting, etc.).

3. While fluency instruction may be foregrounded temporarily to provide support for readers, it must not be the primary focus for long. Readers need expansive, powerful reading practices that always move beyond one particular "resource" within the larger five-part framework.

Fluency assessments should drive instruction; therefore, how often you assess a student's fluency depends on what information you need to provide meaningful, targeted instruction.

WHAT TEACHERS CAN DO: TURN-AROUND STRATEGIES TO SUPPORT FLUENCY

After using a variety of assessments to get to know Cassidy better as an oral reader, Ms. Matthews, with Cassidy, completed a Powerful Reading Plan (see Figure 4.2). Together they identified goals, and Ms. Matthews aligned her reading instruction. To help readers such as Cassidy become more fluent, teachers can do the following:

- Help students choose texts they can read with 95% to 98% accuracy.
- Explicitly model and support the following:
  Reading in appropriate phrases (two to four words at a time)
  Reading with expression
  Changing voices for characters, narrators, and so on
  Appropriately pausing at punctuation

- Utilize the following practices:
  Echo reading (you read one passage or page, then the reader repeats it, attempting to use your fluency practices) to get a sense of a new text
  Choral reading to gain confidence with a text
  Using whisper phones (or plastic piping that can be held like a telephone with one open end at the mouth and one open end at the ear) to encourage listening to one's own reading

There are many other ways teachers can help readers build fluency in whole-group or small-group settings, such as the activities described below.

Reader's Theater

A popular instructional strategy for fluency growth, Reader's Theater is equally embraced by students in early and later elementary grades. In Reader's Theater, students select, write, or are given

FIGURE 4.2. Powerful Reading Plan

(completed by student and teacher)

Date of plan: *January*

I, *Cassidy Stone*, plan to grow my reading practices, and over the next month I am going to focus on:

Reading more smoothly and with more speed.

To reach this goal, I plan to:

1. *Perform a Reader's Theater with Eli, Kelley, and Matt.*

2. *Bring in a favorite poem and practice it to share with the class during share time.*

3. *Make poems on tape for my kindergarten reading buddy.*

I, *Ms. Matthews*, plan to help you grow your reading practices, and over the next month I am going to focus on:

Not interrupting you or correcting you when you read aloud.

Giving you plenty of fun opportunities to read aloud in class.

To help you reach this goal, I will:

1. *Help you perform a Reader's Theater with a small group.*

2. *Help you choose and practice your reading of a poem and time to share with the class.*

3   *Model fluent reading with the whole class and encourage students not to interrupt one another during read-alouds (and practice what I preach!).*

4. *Allow you to use the tape recorder and microphone during independent reading and project time so you can create a book on tape or poems on tape for your kindergarten reading buddy.*

Date of reflection: *February*

Student reflection on the goal(s) above: *I had fun doing the play with my group and reading the poem. I thought I read with expression and changed my voice for the characters. I think my kindergarten buddy loved his poems, and I really think my friends liked the poem I read. I am a faster reader because I try not to look at my teacher and my friends when I'm reading.*

FIGURE 4.2. *continued*

Teacher reflection on the goal(s) above: *Cassidy's fluency has improved, and her awareness of fluent practices in reading has increased dramatically. There is indication of this on the three separate 60-second read-alouds I conducted and also in the qualitative fluency assessments I have done in the past several weeks. Part of the reason for this, I believe, is that she has been able to select texts to read, reread, and rehearse for performance for people who are very important to her (her buddy and her classmates), and she found those texts to be very interesting. Though I will continue to provide opportunities for her to perform oral readings, this will be a secondary area of emphasis; she and I will confer soon about what will be the primary goal in the upcoming month. However, it is clear that Cassidy is highly motivated when she chooses texts that are interesting to her and when she has a purpose for the reading that is intrinsically motivating.*

a piece of text (in any genre or about any topic, including content-area studies) that is separated into different roles for reading. Students often find texts about social justice issues (issues of race, social class, gender, civil rights, workers' rights, children's rights, students' rights) to be particularly powerful and motivating if they know they can potentially influence their audience members to think or behave differently.

Provide students with time to practice and rehearse in school as well as perform before their classmates, other classes, or adults from home and the community. The beauty of Reader's Theater is that students reread and rehearse, which help build fluency, and they have an authentic purpose (performance for an audience) for reading aloud and adjusting volume, rate, intonation, and expression appropriately. Reader's Theater can also be turned into a videotaping or podcasting experience for students, giving them a wider audience beyond the four walls of the classroom.

Repeated Reading for a Tape-Recorded Performance

Repeated reading also leads to more fluent reading. When Ms. Matthews suggested that Cassidy tape-record poems to work on her fluency, Cassidy decided to make poems on tape for her reading buddy in kindergarten. With high motivation, Cassidy read, reread, tape-recorded, and rerecorded the poems numerous times until they sounded "just right" and her reading buddy could follow along

> ## Working with English Language Learners
>
> - Provide ebooks or books on tape that are interesting to students so they can *listen* to a model of a fluent reader in English and practice reading aloud in similar ways.
> - Group students with both native and nonnative English speakers to practice fluency with a variety of texts.
> - Provide bilingual books (or work with students to create bilingual books) and opportunities to reread and perform in students' native languages as well as English.
> - Use (or create) short texts, poems, or songs in English for students to reread and rehearse for an oral performance, such as an open-mic night at school, a poetry slam during lunchtime, or an event celebrating the spoken word.
> - Use online resources (*www.howjsay.com*), handheld talking dictionaries, and peers for pronunciation assistance.

with the text. Selecting poems from *Poetry for Young People: Langston Hughes* (Roessel & Rampersad, 2006) offered Cassidy the opportunity to read poems that were written in a dialect similar to her own ("Mother to Son") as well as ones written in more academic dialects ("Dream Variations"). Additionally, and not unimportantly, these poems offered Cassidy opportunities to think, speak, and address issues of race throughout history and in contemporary times.

So Many Possibilities . . .

It is important to build on a range of resources to connect with students' lives and capitalize on the many types of texts that surround children in their everyday worlds. Some other fluency activities include these:

- Ripped from the headlines (creating weekly newscasts using texts from local and national newspapers)
- Reading comic strips (rehearsing and reading aloud from favorite comic strips during weekly sharing time)
- Reenacting a favorite film trailer (writing a short introduction to promote a new movie or favorite book and reading it aloud to the class)
- Creating podcasts of favorite poems, speeches, or other texts to be posted online

HOW THE TURN-AROUND IMPACTED CASSIDY

With Ms. Matthews's support, Cassidy improved her fluency, self-confidence, and identity as a reader.

- Cassidy realized she needed to reread and practice her fluency if she was expected to read aloud. Ms. Matthews gave her passages in advance so she could practice and be successful.
- Cassidy read her favorite Langston Hughes poem in front of the class. She read with confidence and expression—and smiled widely as the class cheered.
- Cassidy created many tapes for her kindergarten buddy to listen to, reading aloud some of her favorite poems and picture books.
- As her confidence grew, Cassidy became more engaged in reading and was given more choice and purpose by explicitly working on fluency in her reading.

CONNECTIONS TO THE FIVE-PART FRAMEWORK

- *Meaning-making:* As students improve their fluency practices, they can also become more familiar with vocabulary and with making connections and disconnections as they read.
- *Text-using:* Using different kinds of texts helps readers learn different ways in which writers and oral readers express themselves. For example, they can learn about free form and various types of poems, thus becoming more conscientious text-users of poetry and comparing the work of a text-user to the work of writing persuasive speeches and performing them orally.
- *Text-analyzing:* Teachers can encourage students to choose texts that inspire them to work on fluency. As they choose texts, teachers can help students explore topics that are important to them, analyze why a message is powerful, and then compare their own explorations with their classmates' explorations of texts that inspire them.
- *Identity-constructing:* As students work toward a more productive identity as a fluent reader, they also begin constructing an identity as readers with certain reading interests and purposes for reading.

Part III

MEANING-MAKING

A Five-Part Framework for Powerful Reading

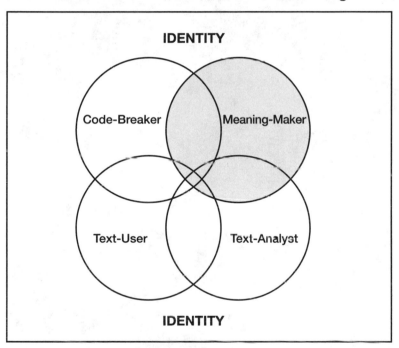

CHAPTER 5

Making Dis/Connections: Practices for Meaning-Making

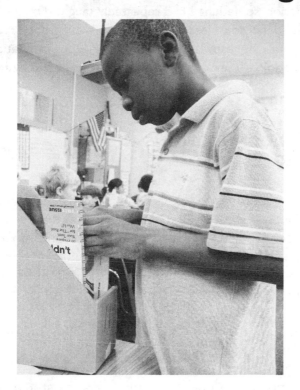

CADENCE: FICTIONALIZING CONNECTIONS TO BE A GOOD READER

Cadence was a talkative White second grader attending an urban school where most children qualified for free or reduced-price lunch. She was an eager reader and began zipping through as many *Henry and Mudge* (Cynthia Rylant) books as she could, impressing her classmates with her fluency and animated expression when she read aloud to some willing listeners. Cadence wasn't necessarily perceived as a reader facing many challenges until one day when I (Stephanie) overheard a "connection" she was making with her book. Cadence was reading *Henry and Mudge and the Best Day of All* (Rylant, 1997), a book about a young boy whose mother and father throw him a birthday party. "I had goldfish at my party, too," Cadence told the students at her table, making a text-to-self connection (Keene & Zimmerman, 2007) that I knew wasn't true. Cadence had had a wonderful birthday party with her mother, her mother's boyfriend, two sisters, a grandma, a stepgrandpa, and a couple neighborhood friends, but her party had not resembled the one portrayed in Rylant's book, and Cadence did not have goldfish at her party. However she *did* articulate a text-to-self connection, something I had repeatedly taught during whole-class, small-group, and individual lessons. In Cadence's mind, good readers did not necessarily talk honestly about their experiences in relation to what they read in books—they made "connections" even if they had to make them up.

THE TROUBLE WITH CONNECTIONS FOR DISCONNECTED READERS

I was teaching second grade when I first read Keene and Zimmerman's *Mosaic of Thought* (2007), which is about the complex work of a reader as she tries to turn the printed word into meaningful thoughts. The authors focused on "connection-making" as a strategy readers use to build meaning. It is a brilliant book that made me nod my head in agreement, thinking, "Yes, of course!" as I read. I flipped over page corners, made notes in the margins, and carried that book around with me for weeks, realizing the tremendous power of connection-making (text-to-self, text-to-text, text-to-world) in teaching reading. Connections were everywhere—I could recognize them, make them myself, and witness my students recognizing and articulating them too.

However, like all fabulous teaching/learning strategies, overemphasizing one way of reading shuts down possibilities for other ways. Surely, focusing on making connections shuts down the possibility of actively making *disconnections*, and I didn't realize the opportunities lost until years later. Many teachers have experienced students making text-to-self connections such as "I have a cat too!" without explaining *why* that connection might be important. And so often the connections are superficial ones instead of the deep, thoughtful, provocative connections we had hoped for. Perhaps students make superficial connections because they perceive that's

> **By the end of this chapter, you will:**
>
> • Understand how connections and disconnections are part of a continuum of meaning-making practices for readers
> • Reflect critically on your teaching of connections and disconnections
> • Have specific tools to support your teaching of connections and disconnections

what "good readers" do and therefore they find *some* way—regardless how meaningless—to articulate connections. Yet exploring the *disconnections* between their experiences and the texts they're reading might really engage them more thoughtfully (Jones & Clarke, 2007). In essence, an overemphasis on connection-making can actually turn students into meaningless connection-makers in their efforts to please. That's hard to swallow as a teacher, but this happens a lot through what is emphasized in reading instruction.

Many readers who are not successful classroom readers are not connected to the purposes, goals, context, and content of school reading. They may be avid readers outside of school, where they can choose what, when, and how they read as well as how they respond to reading, but in school many of them feel disconnected. Though there are infinite reasons for disconnecting from school reading, some are common:

- The language of the school text (English in most cases) is not the dominant or preferred language of the reader.
- Readers cannot find themselves inside the texts at school but instead find lots of books about *other* people's lives.
- Activities readers are asked to do with their texts don't seem interesting or relevant.
- Choice of genre and topic is limited and includes texts enjoyed by the teacher but not by students.
- Readers cannot find meaningful ways to connect with characters, plots, settings, or information in texts.
- Readers perceive reading as an assignment rather than an opportunity.
- Text vocabulary and complexity are too challenging and discourage the reader (or, on the flip side, restrictions on "level" of books allowed to be read leave a student with a book that is perceived as too "babyish").

TEACHER EXERCISE:
THINKING ABOUT YOUR OWN DISCONNECTIONS

Think about books, movies, advertisements, and other texts that you feel disconnected from.

- How does it feel to disconnect? What does it make you think? Wonder?
- What if you felt completely disconnected from the contexts, plots, and characters of science fiction books but those were all you were allowed to read each day? What kind of identity would you build as a reader? What kinds of reading practices would you find meaningful?

Ironically, one powerful way to reengage students can be to encourage them to articulate their *disconnections* from the texts they're reading.

THINKING CRITICALLY ABOUT CLASSROOM PRACTICE: DO YOU ENCOURAGE MAKING BOTH CONNECTIONS AND DISCONNECTIONS?

Nearly every teacher we know focuses—heavily—on making connections. These instructional practices begin in pre-K and move across the K–12 spectrum in the United States. We are not implying that making connections is wrong. What we do want all teachers to consider, however, is whether *disconnections* are being explicitly taught alongside connections. As every good researcher knows, insightful learning often comes from outlying examples or counterintuitive perspectives. Yet, by focusing on making connections, teachers may very well be encouraging readers to habitually connect with the familiar (if possible) and ignore powerful differences. Before I could imagine what to turn around to make this situation better for Cadence, I had to reconsider my classroom practices, as you may want to do, using the following questions:

- Do I model connection-making practices more than disconnection-making ones?
- Do I provide reading materials that allow all students to make meaningful connections with the lives and contexts portrayed in the texts?

- Do I read aloud books to explore text-to-self, text-to-text, and text-to-world disconnections?
- Do I use disconnections as opportunities for students to explore social, economic, and ecological injustices in the world?
- Do I use disconnections as opportunities for students to critically consider how publishers portray lives in books and who benefits from those portrayals?
- Do I validate readers' connections more than their disconnections?
- Do I make assumptions about readers' connections and disconnections with certain texts, or do I ask open-ended questions to learn more about their perspectives?
- Do I encourage students to listen to, respect, and learn from all readers' connections and disconnections even when they represent conflicting perspectives?
- Do I privilege my own connections with books in a way that may make students uncomfortable voicing their disconnections?
- Do I demonstrate enthusiasm for text-to-text disconnections that challenge what we, as a class, thought we knew about a topic?
- Do I remind students that all knowledge is *partial* and that we learn and grow when faced with information that challenges what we used to know?

GETTING TO KNOW STUDENTS WELL: CAN THEY FIND THEIR LIVES REPRESENTED IN CLASSROOM TEXTS?

Cadence was a competitive swimmer on a summer team; played outside with her sisters and friends after school; and wrote long stories about her family, whom she loved very much—all parts of her life that could provide potential connections with some children's books in school. But given that most books found in classrooms portray idealized lives filled with economic security, spacious living quarters, and smiling, carefree adults and children, Cadence's disconnections from school texts were probably more powerful and overwhelming than her connections.

Cadence's father had been incarcerated since shortly after her birth, and her mother worked two full-time jobs to make ends meet. Cadence and her sisters alternated among her grandmother's home, her stepgrandfather's home, and neighbors' homes for playing, eating, sleeping, and doing homework. During the 4 years I knew Cadence, her family's apartment had burned down and they had lost everything, her mother had lost her driver's license due to unpaid fines, living arrangements were constantly being negotiated, and money was always—always—very tight.

No wonder Cadence had to fictionalize her own life to make connections with books in the *Henry and Mudge* series. She must have wondered how her own life mattered in school, where she constantly read books about children who lived lives very different from her own. Is that what childhood is *supposed* to be like? If so, what does that say about *my* childhood? It must be very complicated indeed for children in school to be constantly faced with idealized versions of family life when they know their real-world experiences don't resemble such portrayals.

WHAT TEACHERS CAN DO: TURN-AROUND STRATEGIES TO ENCOURAGE DIS/CONNECTIONS

Cadence needed a turn-around, a way to articulate her disconnections from texts and to question and critique the overrepresentation of such lives, a way to reposition herself and her own life as valuable and validated in school. But the process had to begin with my own turn-around of classroom practices.

Simple Practices to Recognize, Value, and Learn from Disconnections

Not Like My Life. Fictional children's texts are powerful tools for telling children and adults what "normal" life should be. Readers who do not connect with mainstream ways of living (as represented in children's books) must be encouraged to articulate their disconnections and to challenge what is considered normal. Readers can mark a simple "NLML" (not like my life) on a sticky note and put it on a page where they experience a strong disconnection with either the text or an illustration. In whole-group share time, small-group conversations, or individual conferences, the reader can articulate how the text/illustration is not like his life, how that makes him feel as a reader, what he would change to make it more like his life, and what issues it makes him think about in the larger society.

Additionally, if students become accustomed to this practice, encourage them to consider who might write "NLML" on the pieces of writing they themselves produce in class—a practice that can promote conscious consideration of multiple perspectives, of how different readers are positioned by writers, and of how those writers are using their power to either promote stereotypes or challenge injustices (see Jones, 2006).

Sticky Words. We see all students in U.S. classrooms as continuing their journeys of learning the English language even if they are native English speakers. Therefore, teachers must recognize when students disconnect from words, phrases, or sentence complexity in the texts they read in school. "Sticky Words" is a simple strategy of students writing a word, phrase, or sentence on a sticky note and placing it on the page where the disconnection is in the text. This practice does two major things:

1. It alerts the reader to her disconnection from unknown words, phrases, or confusing sentences so she doesn't get into the habit of reading "over" unknown language.
2. It provides a specific talking point for the reader to ask her reading partner and the teacher about.

A classroom may also have a Sticky Words chart or bulletin board where students add words/phrases/sentences and sketches or definitions once they've inquired about the meaning of unknown language in their text.

Quick Sketch for Dis/Connections. For a "Quick Sketch," students would use a T-chart, with "Connections" on one side and "Disconnections" on the other side of the chart. Readers would use this chart to quickly sketch pictures of events or topics in their texts that they connect with and disconnect from during their reading; this practice encourages readers to recognize that they both connect and disconnect during their reading. It also serves as a conversation starter with a reading partner or teacher during share time or individual conferences.

Dis/Connection Webs. A Dis/Connection Web (see Figure 5.1) also encourages readers to pay attention to both connections and disconnections, but it prompts readers one step further than *recognizing* them. Readers write their dis/connections in the circles on the web, then elaborate in the rectangles on what each dis/connection makes them *wonder about, think about, want to research,* or *wish the author had done differently.* In other words, the Dis/Connection Web pushes readers not only to make dis/connections but also to consider why those dis/connections matter and how they can plan future reading based on their wonderings.

FIGURE 5.1. Dis/Connection Web

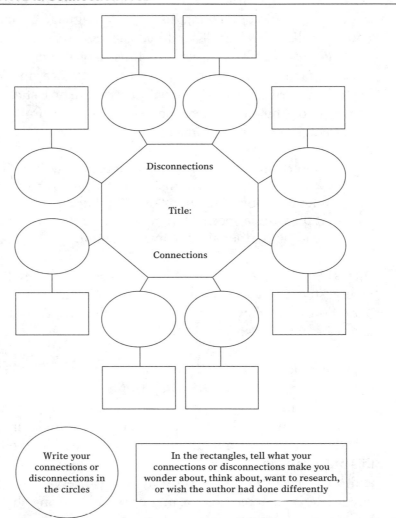

FIGURE 5.2. Challenge-That-Text!

Name: _____ Date: _____

Text I read: _____

This text makes you think or believe . . .	But I found other texts that make me think differently . . .

Challenge-That-Text! Tables. A "Challenge-That-Text!" table (see Figure 5.2) encourages students to find disconnections (text-to-self, text-to-text, or text-to-world) and become stronger text analysts. Challenge-That-Text! tables can be used to challenge the following:

- Stereotypes represented in texts (gender roles; family structures; children's lives; and issues of immigration, race, social class, religion, language, sexuality, etc.)
- Disconfirming evidence across texts (e.g., some texts portraying Christopher Columbus as an "explorer" and others containing historical evidence of indigenous people being massacred and/or removed from their land and families)
- Taken-for-granted perspectives in "world texts" (e.g., students can search for texts that recognize the economic inequities in our society and question the assumption that being "poor" in the United States means you are lazy or have a bad life and that being "rich" means you work hard and have a good life)

More Opportunities for Powerful Connection-Making

1. Take a "You Be the Teacher" trip to the school library or public library, where students can select books and other reading materials they would like to see in the classroom library. Check those out under your name and add them to the classroom library for independent reading.

2. Develop your classroom library in areas of high interest for your students (TV series books, graphic novels, comic books, horror fiction, nonfiction books about their interests, realistic fiction books about characters and settings they can relate to, song lyric books, contemporary poetry, local newspapers, etc.).
3. Allow access to the Internet during independent reading/ work time.
4. Publish and use students' writing as reading texts during independent reading time.

HOW THE TURN-AROUND IMPACTED CADENCE

Cadence seemed to transform immediately after I introduced the notion of disconnections, and we prepared her Powerful Reading Plan (see Figure 5.3). In her initial exploration of disconnections, she flipped feverishly through pages of *Henry and Mudge* books, talking about how the family sits together at dinnertime and how her family sits in the living room to eat because they don't have a dinner table. She critiqued a frilly-dressed girl in the book as not representing girls she knows—girls who think it's too "stuck up" to wear fancy dresses all the time or who only wear a fancy dress around the Christmas or Easter holidays. Then we talked about what kind

Working with English Language Learners

- Use "Sticky Words" to encourage readers to recognize and talk about disconnections and connections with words and concepts.
- Provide texts (audio and print) in the reader's native language.
- Provide bilingual texts (audio and print) and have students draw, write, or discuss the connections and disconnections between the two different texts.
- Provide access to texts portraying different kinds of immigration experiences and encourage dis/connections.
- Read aloud texts that represent the complexity of acquiring more than one language in different contexts (e.g., *Marianthe's Story: Painted Words and Spoken Memories* [Aliki, 1998]) and encourage dis/connections.

FIGURE 5.3. Powerful Reading Plan

(completed by student and teacher)

Date of plan: *January*

I, *Cadence*, plan to grow my reading practices, and over the next month I am going to focus on:

> *Talking about how my family life is different from the characters in the books and noticing when I don't have connections but I do have disconnections with my reading.*

To reach this goal, I plan to:

> 1. *Try a Challenge-That-Text! table to challenge how kids and families are in books and in real life.*
>
> 2. *Do a Quick Sketch of my connections and disconnections in my reading notebook when I read new books.*

I, *Stephanie Jones*, plan to help you grow your reading practices, and over the next month I am going to focus on:

> *Helping you challenge how families and kids are in books and real life and finding more reading materials for the classroom library that you can connect with.*

To help you reach this goal, I will:

> 1. *Teach the whole class practices to learn from disconnections as well as connections.*
>
> 2. *Confer with you about your disconnections when reading and your Challenge-That-Text! project.*
>
> 3. *Help you publish the writing you're doing in writing workshop so we can put those in the classroom library for you and others to read.*
>
> 4. *Demonstrate* Not Like My Life, Quick Sketches, Sticky Words, *and* Challenge-That-Text! *tables for the whole class.*

Date of reflection: *February*

Student reflections on the goal(s) above: *I never knew about disconnections before, but now it's a lot of fun to notice the disconnections and talk about them with my friends and teacher, and even sketch about them in my notebook. Now I really see that book authors are always sending messages to readers and some readers will connect with the messages and some readers won't. Or you might connect with some of it and disconnect with other parts.*

Teacher reflections on the goal(s) above: *I never knew how much I emphasized connection-making before I did this with Cadence. Now my teaching has really changed and I'm always asking students to consider both connections and disconnections—a whole range of possible responses to a reading. This has also made me rethink some of my other prompts, like "what was your favorite part?" which actually corners a reader into having a favorite part rather than not liking a text, or having many enjoyable parts but not wanting to state one as a favorite. I'm thinking more about how my teaching can corner students and how to work against that.*

of lives the author and illustrator might have had to influence their words and pictures. Cadence and her classmates decided to write books for kids that represent their kind of "normal" life. To begin, we all walked around the school and surrounding neighborhood to take photographs of what they perceived as normal in their lives, including things they enjoyed and things they wanted to change. Together they selected their own texts (photographs, poems, non-narrative informational pieces, personal narratives, and book reviews) to show in a public (classroom) gallery and self-publish in a literary magazine in order to present pictures of their normal lives that were not typically found in children's books.

I also worked hard to find published texts that provided more opportunities for Cadence to make connections, including books about having a parent in jail (e.g., *Amber Was Brave, Essie Was Smart* [Williams, 2001], a book that quickly became a classroom favorite) and girl characters who do not fit traditional gender stereotypes (see additional book suggestions in the Appendix). This turn-around not only positioned Cadence as a more powerful reader who was valued for the disconnections she shared in class; it also set her on a trajectory of valuing herself and her life experiences in a society where we are always told what to desire and idealize. It turned me around, too, as someone who should have known what it was like never to find yourself in a book and the damaging effects of such a predicament.

CONNECTIONS TO THE FIVE-PART FRAMEWORK

- *Identity-constructing*: It is empowering for readers to have space for articulating disconnections. This power can position readers more actively in their reading and motivate them to engage with texts they don't find particularly interesting or well written.
- *Text-analyzing*: Readers who find disconnections are in a good position to recognize discrepancies between texts, leading to critical analysis of authors' perspectives and purposes. Challenge-That-Text! can get readers excited about challenging the usually taken-for-granted-authority of published texts.
- *Code-breaking*: Using Sticky Words can refocus a reader's attention on unknown words, word parts, and unusual spelling patterns.

CHAPTER 6

Vocabulary:
A Meaning-Making Resource

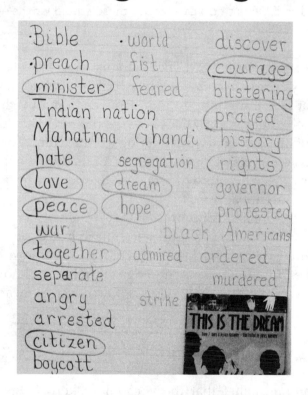

GARY: RESISTING "THESE STUPID WORDS"

Gary was one of a fifth-grade group who met with me (Lane) every day for about 40 minutes in my reading intervention program. His teacher, Mr. Fitzgerald, had asked me to assist these students with reading their whole-class text, *My Side of the Mountain* (Craighead George, 1959). Each day, the students came with the book and a long list of vocabulary words that the teacher wanted them to define. He had chosen words that might prove difficult, and they were supposed to look up the words and write their definitions before reading the chapter. So we settled into a routine where we spent about 25 minutes defining vocabulary words, then, if we were lucky, a few minutes actually reading. It did not take long for me to recognize the negative impact this routine was having on Gary. He regularly forgot to bring his pencil, book, or notebook and had to take the time to go back to his classroom to retrieve the forgotten object. Not long afterwards, Gary would start to act out and disrupt others in the group. Frustrated by the power Gary was using in the group to distract us all, I finally got angry and told him that he needed to work on his vocabulary words in order to do well in Mr. Fitzgerald's class. He looked at me and said, "What do I care about these stupid words—they mean nothing to me!"

Of course, Gary was right. That daily list of preselected vocabulary words from a book in which he had no interest did not mean anything to him. He was bored by the repetitiveness of looking up words every day, he did not relate to any of the words, and the dictionary did nothing to entice him. Furthermore, Gary was learning that he was the type of reader who had to define long lists of words before he even got to open the text—not a positive reading identity.

Students cannot make meaning from text if they do not know the words, but providing meaningful vocabulary instruction goes far beyond defining a list of words. Instruction that will turn readers around to be more motivated and engaged relies on knowing students well and using this knowledge to plan effective meaning-making instruction.

VOCABULARY AS A MEANING-MAKING RESOURCE

It is a long-standing belief that the vocabulary knowledge of a reader directly correlates to the ability to comprehend a text (Davis, 1944). This seems to be common sense—you need to know what words mean, or at least approximate an unfamiliar word's meaning, in order to fully understand a text. This connection has been demonstrated in the research literature over the years (Fitzgerald & Graves, 2004) and is highly correlated with school success (Hart & Risley, 2003). However, we want to remind you that *all* understanding falls on a spectrum and even knowing the definitions of words will not guarantee a rich reading. Additionally, readers *can* engage meaningfully with texts without knowing the meanings of each word.

> **BY THE END OF THIS CHAPTER, YOU WILL:**
>
> • Understand why vocabulary is an important meaning-making resource
> • Critically analyze your vocabulary instruction
> • Have specific tools to help you learn about your students' vocabulary so as to design meaningful instruction
> • Have specific suggestions for instruction in vocabulary that is purposeful and results in meaningful reading engagement

Michael F. Graves (2006, 2008), a leading vocabulary expert, establishes that there should be four parts to any vocabulary program: providing rich and varied language experiences, teaching individual words, teaching word-learning strategies, and fostering word consciousness. Clearly, vocabulary instruction is a multifaceted and deep process and cannot be boiled down to a simple how-to list, but all good instruction starts with the teacher and the student.

THINKING CRITICALLY ABOUT CLASSROOM PRACTICE: HOW DO YOU TEACH VOCABULARY?

Gary's teacher had good intentions with his vocabulary assignment, but this instruction did not go beyond an individual word approach. The listed words did not help students develop an engaged word consciousness, and although using a dictionary is a valid word-learning strategy, it is not always the most helpful method, especially as a young reader pores over a short novel. It is important to remember that vocabulary involves meaning-making and must go hand in hand with real reading. If this does not happen, then vocabulary instruction can be ineffective and lead to disengaged readers like Gary. To assist Gary, I helped Mr. Fitzgerald examine his vocabulary instruction to find places for a turn-around. You can use the following questions to examine your own approach to teaching vocabulary:

- Do I cultivate a culture of curiosity around words in my classroom?
- Do my students spend more time on vocabulary than on actual reading?

- Do I teach vocabulary as part of the reading process or as a separate category?
- Do I preassess what words my students already know about a topic before reading?
- Do I engage in vocabulary work at a variety of points during the reading process, such as *before, during*, and *after* reading?
- Do I spontaneously teach vocabulary across the day?
- Do I confer with students about vocabulary acquisition?
- Do I connect words the students don't know to words that they do know?
- Do I teach words, or do I help students discover words?
- Do I model word-learning strategies through my read-alouds?
- Do I celebrate my students' unique vocabulary knowledge?

GETTING TO KNOW STUDENTS WELL: WHAT IS THEIR WORD KNOWLEDGE?

Gary had recently transferred to this suburban school from a larger city school district when he moved in with his grandmother. His personal life was in upheaval, and his academic life was not faring much better. Gary was comfortable reading simpler works than the assigned book, which likely contributed to the perception that he was having difficulty with attention and behavior. Gary was identified as a "struggling reader," but this label was doing nothing other than getting him some outside assistance that wasn't producing positive results. In order for Mr. Fitzgerald to turn things around for Gary, he needed to get to know him as a person and as a meaning-maker. By getting to know Gary's reading habits, interests, and strengths, Mr. Fitzgerald could gain some powerful insight on how to turn his instruction around and help Gary become more engaged as a reader.

Getting to Know Gary's Word Strategies

Vocabulary instruction includes developing independent word strategies for learning new words within the practice of reading. The best way to assess a student's word strategies is through a one-to-one conference. Mr. Fitzgerald selected a short piece of text with some difficult words and sat with Gary as he read it. When Gary stumbled over unfamiliar words, Mr. Fitzgerald asked him, "What do you think this word means?" and "What clues did you use to guess what this word means?" By conferring with Gary about his meaning-making practices for vocabulary, Mr. Fitzgerald learned that Gary was using word parts (root words, prefixes, suffixes), and together they decided to make that one of Gary's goals in his Powerful Reading Plan (see Figure 6.1).

Getting to Know Students' Specific Word Knowledge

One way to get to know students' word knowledge is to have each student choose a topic that is important to him or her and generate relevant vocabulary to create a personal word web. The teacher displays these webs in the room in order to use each student as a resident expert in a particular area. All students have a rich reservoir of vocabulary knowledge relating to something, and accessing these personal word webs—even those not school-related—celebrates a student's word knowledge and can be used to make connections with future academic-based vocabulary. For example, Gary had a passion and rich vocabulary knowledge around basketball. Gary's word web included *offensive, swingman, flagrant, possession, substitute,* and so on. Capitalizing on Gary's rich vocabulary knowledge about basketball provided a bridge to other words studied in the class that year, and it made him the resident expert on all things basketball.

TEACHER EXERCISE:
THINKING ABOUT YOUR OWN WORD STRATEGIES

Find a text that is challenging for you:

1. Skim a passage and list any words that are unfamiliar.
2. Read the passage and pay attention to these words. Did you figure out their meaning as you read? What meaning-making practices did you use?
3. Now make a list of words from the text that you still don't know. What tools could you use to learn the meanings of these words? Is it imperative to know these meanings, or is your understanding of the text sufficient?
4. Do your practices in items 2 and 3 reflect the kind of vocabulary teaching you do in your classroom?

FIGURE 6.1. Powerful Reading Plan

(completed by student and teacher)

Date of plan: *September*

I, *Gary Jenkins*, plan to grow my reading practices, and over the next month I am going to focus on:

> *Learning more vocabulary to help me understand the books I'm reading better.*

To reach this goal, I plan to:

1. *Use Post-it notes to mark prefixes and suffixes in my reading and to talk about them with my reading partner or my teacher.*

2. *Start a vocabulary journal to connect new words to words I already know.*

I, *Mr. Fitzgerald*, plan to help you grow your reading practices, and over the next month I am going to focus on:

> *Helping you grow your word knowledge through prefixes and suffixes.*

> *Using more engaging strategies in my own teaching beyond vocabulary lists.*

To help you reach this goal, I will:

1. *Help you keep a vocabulary journal of word parts and connecting new words to words you already know.*

2. *Create self-rating checklists for the whole-class readings we will do.*

3. *Start a "sesquipedalian chart" for the class to add long, unusual, and interesting words.*

4. *Point out my vocabulary strategies as I read aloud.*

Date of reflection: *November*

Student reflection on the goal(s) above: *I started a vocabulary journal, where I made a word web for our unit on tropical rainforest and learned many new words such as* understory, omnivore, deforestation, *and* indigenous. *I have a lot of other new words in my vocabulary journal, too. I did a self-rating sheet on our next unit on weather and made a plan for how I was going to learn the words that I didn't know and teach them to other students. I'm paying more attention to prefixes and suffixes in my reading and my writing, too.*

Teacher reflection on the goal(s) above: *I made a point to be more direct in my read-alouds when I came to a new word to demonstrate my word-learning strategies. I had conferences with Gary about his vocabulary journal and his noticings around prefixes and suffixes in his reading. We started a sesquipedalian chart that has become popular with a lot of students in the classroom—they're all looking for words that can be added to the chart, and they love the idea of being sesquipedalians. I really notice a difference in how the students are using new vocabulary; it seems a lot more interesting to them and to me than our vocabulary lists that I used to do.*

Making Vocabulary More Meaningful

There are times in the curriculum when we need students to learn specific word meanings, particularly when studying specific content. Mr. Fitzgerald insisted on teaching *My Side of the Mountain*, but the students were not motivated in the way that he had hoped. Therefore, we did two things to make this unit more meaningful:

1. We situated the reading of this book within a broader study of environmentalism and its effects on our lives. By pairing this novel with social, political, and economic issues around land use, conservation, our dependence on nature, and the policies of deforestation, the students became more intrigued by and invested in their reading.
2. We combined this approach with an investigative approach to vocabulary. Students self-selected difficult words to present to the class, kept a word journal, and contributed to a bulletin board of words related to environmentalism.

Gary, and the others, began to care more about "these stupid words," especially as they related to a broader context. However, Mr. Fitzgerald still had certain words he wanted students to know, so he used a self-rating checklist (see Figure 6.2). This checklist presents students with a list of words and asks them to rate their current understanding of a word. This helps the students to become more conscious of their specific word knowledge and encourages them to create a plan to get to know specific words better. For

FIGURE 6.2. Self-Rating Checklist for Vocabulary

Word	I know this word well	I have seen or heard this word	I don't know this word at all
forage			X
eddy			X
conservationist		X	
survival	X		

Plan for learning these words:

I will look up forage *and* eddy *in the dictionary and use context clues to help me better understand* conservationist.

example, before reading one chapter of *My Side of the Mountain*, Mr. Fitzgerald gave Gary this self-rating checklist. Using this checklist, Gary came up with a plan to learn the words that he didn't know well. This helped Gary take some ownership of and pride in his meaning-making and see himself as a word learner rather than someone who goes through the motions of finding definitions to someone else's important words.

WHAT TEACHERS CAN DO: TURN-AROUND STRATEGIES TO GROW VOCABULARY

Assessing and understanding Gary as a meaning-maker who has rich vocabulary knowledge—even if it is not school-based—was the first step in helping turn around Gary's identity as a reader. However, just assessing his knowledge was not good enough; Mr. Fitzgerald needed to have multiple instructional strategies to help Gary grow as a reader as well as enhance the meaning-making abilities of all his students. There are many ways to acquire new vocabulary, and we provide a quick list of some of the activities that a teacher who has a student like Gary might want to use based on what Mr. Fitzgerald learned about Gary. It is important to note, however, that the foundation for building meaning-making resources was to let Gary read something that was interesting to him. Situating *My Side of the Mountain* within a broader context helped Gary see a purpose to this reading and become more excited about it. Letting students self-select texts, however, is also important to support readers as they develop more powerful vocabulary and reading practices.

Vocabulary Journal

With year-long vocabulary journals, students become collectors of personal/social words, content words, words they want to know, and words they are still unsure of. This will lead not only to increasing individual word knowledge but also to developing word consciousness.

Word Webs Across Content Areas

Using word webs across content areas is important. The study of genre in writing, fossil fuels in science, measurement in mathematics,

---

WORKING WITH ENGLISH LANGUAGE LEARNERS

- Encourage students to make personal word webs in their native language and in English.
- Create a word wall that incorporates words from all languages spoken by students in the classroom.
- If appropriate, demonstrate the use of a double-sided vocabulary journal—one side for English and the other for the corresponding word or concept in their native languages.
- Provide students with English texts at their reading levels, and encourage them to recognize and mark unfamiliar vocabulary that will become a part of their self-selected vocabulary work.
- If a student speaks a Latin-based language like English, engage the whole class and/or small groups in a Latin inquiry to help everyone recognize similarities and differences among root words.

---

or famous people in history provides great opportunities to generate multiple layers of word knowledge specific to the unit of inquiry. If students are engaged in vocabulary work throughout the day and the year, they will be able to make connections between vocabulary and meaning-making with all texts.

Inquiry-Based Word Study

By engaging in word study activities such as word sorts, word walls, and making words, the perspective shifts from prescriptive to more of an inquiry approach. Word study helps students become inquisitive about words and engage in vocabulary more actively.

Read-Alouds

Teachers should read aloud from a variety of texts to expose students to many different words. However, it is not always enough to "expose" students to new words this way—a teacher should acknowledge the new word, discuss it or lead an inquiry around it, and add it to the growing classroom chart/bulletin board on interesting words. Students can also have Post-it notes on which they can jot down "cool" or "interesting" words when they hear them in a read-aloud.

Self-Selection of Words

Allowing students to choose words to learn as they read—and how to learn them—is another powerful strategy. Students can pick words to learn and teach their classmates some of their words (through dramatic performance, skits, drawing, word associations, etc.). This strategy, rather than just giving them a word list, lets students have control over learning words and will increase their motivation.

HOW THE TURN-AROUND IMPACTED GARY

By the end of the schoolyear, Gary had developed some powerful practices around vocabulary:

- He used prefixes and suffixes more as he figured out word meanings of unknown words.
- He became a word collector through his vocabulary journal.
- He was able to connect words he already knew to new words.
- He developed more word consciousness and often contributed sticky notes of new words to the class word charts.

Overall, Gary became more engaged in class and with school in general, and he started to construct an identity as a word learner, a reader, and a meaning-maker.

CONNECTIONS TO THE FIVE-PART FRAMEWORK

- *Code-breaking:* By focusing on root words and affixes, students are engaged in both code-breaking and meaning-making.
- *Text-using:* Students can use text features to help identify words they didn't know and as a resource for figuring out meaning. For example, in nonfiction books, students can recognize bold and italicized print as a clue about words that may be challenging.
- *Text-analyzing:* By situating individual books within larger social or political units, students can read critically and think about issues of power in the text and in society.

Part IV

TEXT-USING

A Five-Part Framework for Powerful Reading

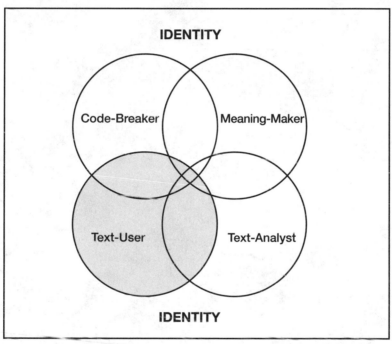

CHAPTER 7

Text-Using Resources: Informational Non-Narrative Texts

It looks like...	We call it...	We find it...	It helps us...
Contents All Together 4 Wind 6 Fire 8 Water 10 The Sun 12 Shaping the Landscape 14 Making Mountains 16 Earthquakes 18 Volcanoes 20 Tsunamis 22 Glossary 24	table of contents	in the front	...find information quickly about a topic ...find the page number for information ... "dive in" and "out" of books
What elephants eat Elephants are enormous and they need to eat a lot of food. When the rainy season, the grass grows tall. African elephants will walk a long way to find it. Long grass is their favorite food.	heading	in the text	...get ready to read the page ...find specific information

JACOB: DISMISSING TEXTS THAT ARE "NOT THAT INTERESTING"

Jacob, a fourth grader, was curious about lots of things in the world and visited the classroom library at least three times a week during the non-fiction unit. It wasn't because he was a voracious reader who immersed himself in books to satisfy his thirst for knowledge. Rather, it was that his attention rarely stayed with a text beyond a few minutes or pages of reading it. He complained that a lot of texts were either "hard to follow" or "not that interesting after all." Once he quickly determined that a book was too confusing or too boring, he returned it to its bin in the classroom library and searched for another one. His teacher, Ms. Carter, worried that if he couldn't stay focused on a single text, he would fall behind in his reading. Her concern was heightened by the upcoming state test, which she knew was full of nonfiction passages. Jacob was already having a difficult time answering basic comprehension questions about these texts, and Ms. Carter wondered if she should just assign him a book to read so he would at least finish something.

Jacob was a student who knew that reading nonfiction texts could be interesting and useful, but he didn't know *how* to read them. Furthermore, since the unit his classroom was focusing on was called "nonfiction," he alternated between reading magazine articles, information books, narrative nonfiction texts, and biographies. What he didn't understand, and what his teacher didn't realize, was that Jacob needed to learn how to identify and use *informational non-narrative texts* for his specific intentions in seeking knowledge. Learning to use different kinds of texts for different purposes helps students understand how to better approach their reading and leads to more powerful reading practices.

READING INFORMATIONAL NON-NARRATIVE TEXTS AS TEXT-USERS

Informational non-narrative texts are just one of the many genres that fall under the large umbrella of nonfiction. Often called *expository texts*, informational non-narrative texts are concerned with presenting facts and explanations without the story elements of character, plot, setting, and dialogue, and they are frequently used in content-area instruction. As children progress through school, their encounters with this genre become more frequent, with informational texts comprising more than 75% of their reading by the time they reach sixth grade and up to 80% of the passages they read on standardized tests (Moss, 2004a, 2004b). But students are not reading enough in this genre, or if they are, they aren't receiving instruction that offers specific strategies for doing so (Dreher, 2003; Harvey & Goudvis, 2007).

By the end of this chapter, you will:

- Understand the features and purposes of informational non-narrative texts and how they help readers become powerful text-users
- Critically reflect on your teaching about the features and purposes of informational texts
- Have specific tools to help you assess students' uses of informational texts in their own lives
- Have specific strategies for teaching students to read informational non-narrative texts that are purposeful and meaningful to them

Many teachers speak of helping students read informational non-narrative texts as reading to learn versus learning to read. Underlying that notion is the assumption that if students know how to read in one genre, they already know how to read in others. However, there are many students like Jacob who find informational non-narrative texts confusing. Many researchers argue that children should be given lots of opportunities to read such texts, as well as receive explicit instruction in reading informational texts as early as the primary grades (Duke, 2004; Pressley, Rankin, & Yokoi, 1996).

Informational non-narrative texts are often constructed in ways that are more reader-friendly than narrative texts. Informational texts follow a predictable structure, with signposts along the way

Teacher Exercise:
Thinking About Your Text-Using Practices

Grab the nearest informational text available to you.

1. Flip through the text from cover to cover. How is it organized? What kind of features does it contain to help you make sense of the layout and overall content of the text (e.g., table of contents, table of charts, headings, italicized print, index, glossary)?
2. Scan one of the chapters or sections. What extra features does the text provide in the margins, in colored boxes, in distinct font?
3. Read one of the pages more carefully. How do you sort through and organize the information?

to help readers figure out where to go if they want to find specific information. Thinking of this genre in this way helps to focus on teaching students to be text-users. Being a text-user means "setting a purpose for reading, understanding that different texts require different types of reading, knowing about and using the various cultural and social functions of texts, and being able to respond to texts in a variety of ways" (Rush, 2004, p. 38). This means that good instruction on reading informational non-narrative texts requires teachers to know their students well and to know what kinds of knowledge-seeking inquiries will help students use these texts in meaningful ways.

THINKING CRITICALLY ABOUT CLASSROOM PRACTICE: WHAT IS YOUR APPROACH TO INFORMATIONAL NON-NARRATIVE TEXTS?

Jacob's teacher, Ms. Carter, knew that her students needed to read a variety of texts to become stronger readers. However, she grouped many genres under the broad umbrella of nonfiction. She didn't realize she needed to provide students with explicit instruction about nonfiction texts—what they are, how to read them, and why someone might want to read them. Assuming that Jacob would already know what do with this genre, how to identify the kinds of informational texts that would be most useful to him, and how to transfer the reading skills he had learned with other genres to this one placed an overwhelming amount of responsibility on him. It also set him up to grow easily frustrated and resistant when he could not figure out why he wasn't learning the kinds of things he hoped to learn from these texts.

Distraught, Ms. Carter considered resorting to assigning Jacob an informational text to read so he would at least be doing the same kinds of reading activities as the rest of the class. However, this approach might have served to further turn him away from reading, causing him to see informational texts as not only confusing or boring but also forced upon him and personally meaningless. What Ms. Carter didn't know was how Jacob used texts in his everyday life. With this knowledge, she could build instruction on what Jacob was already doing well, helping him make connections about how to transfer those skills to his reading work. To help Ms. Carter turn around her instruction, she needed to think critically about her current practice using the following questions, which can also help you examine your approach to nonfiction instruction:

- Do I lump all kinds of texts together into one generic "nonfiction" category, or do I draw students' attention to the different structures and formats that nonfiction can entail? (Types of nonfiction include magazines, textbooks, biographies, newspapers, websites, recipes, timelines, etc.)
- Do I provide explicit instruction about the purposes, features, and perspectives that are involved in non-narrative informational texts?
- Do I provide enough of these texts on a variety of topics that my students are interested in?
- Do I confer with individual students about the specific knowledge they hope to gain from reading informational non-narrative texts?
- Do I assign all students the same texts to read, or do I help them to make meaningful and purposeful choices about the informational non-narrative texts they read?
- Do I know anything about how students are already using these kinds of texts in their lives so I can build on these strengths?

Thinking critically about how informational non-narrative texts currently fit into your reading instruction can help you see the cracks in your teaching so you can begin to turn it around. Another step, of course, is to learn about who your students are as people, readers, and learners in order to make sure you are working to meet students' needs.

GETTING TO KNOW STUDENTS WELL: HOW DO THEY USE INFORMATIONAL TEXTS?

Jacob was a charismatic young boy who easily captured audiences of classmates with his energy and good humor. He also had a personal passion for anything related to outer space and spent lots of time outside of school watching television documentaries and science fiction movies, visiting museums and planetariums with his family, and looking up information about space exploration on the Internet.

Not knowing these details about Jacob, Ms. Carter was leaning toward describing him as a struggling reader. After all, he seemed uninterested and unfocused when reading the informational texts available to him. In reality, he was lost not only about what kinds of information texts would serve his inquiries but also about how to read them strategically to find the information he wanted to know.

Surveying Text Use

One of the quickest ways to learn about students' perceptions of informational non-narrative texts is to have them complete a survey about their current interactions with the genre. The answers that students provide can be useful for assessing whether the kinds of texts that are available in the classroom are ones with which they are already familiar. You can use the following questions to survey your students:

1. What are some topics you're interested in learning about? What do you already know about them?
2. How do you usually find out information about those topics?
3. What kinds of texts do you usually go to when you want to find out more information about something?
4. What do you find helpful about those texts?
5. What makes those texts hard to figure out?

From Jacob's text-user survey, Ms. Carter discovered that Jacob was interested in outer space and that he regularly used TV listings, movie reviews, and Internet websites to help fuel his inquiries. She also learned that he had a decent knowledge of reading charts and graphs.

Assessing Concepts About Text Structure

A text structure assessment resembles the surveys that primary grade teachers use to determine emergent readers' concepts about print. However, this survey asks a student about using the index, scanning headings, and locating introductions. To complete such a survey, choose an informational non-narrative text and sit down with the student to ask the following questions:

1. What is this text about?
2. Is it divided into different sections? Where could you find out if it is? What are those sections?
3. (After looking at a table of contents or index) If I wanted to read about ___, where would I find it in this text?
4. If the text didn't have headings, what else could I use to help me figure out what it is about?
5. (Point to a figure or picture) How can I find out what this is about?
6. (Point to any extra text in the margins) What do I do with this?
7. How can I use the text to help me decide what's important to read and what I could ignore?

After Ms. Carter sat down with Jacob and asked him questions about text structure, she realized that he approached this genre as if he were reading narrative texts, expecting them to follow predictable, linear structures that would explain everything he wanted to know. He also flipped through pages randomly until he found the information he sought.

Knowing these details about Jacob helped Ms. Carter figure out that Jacob needed to know how to use informational non-narrative texts so he could read them in powerful ways.

WHAT TEACHERS CAN DO: TURN-AROUND STRATEGIES TO DEVELOP READING OF INFORMATIONAL TEXTS WITH PURPOSE AND MEANING

Knowledge about Jacob's reading interests and interactions around this genre helped Ms. Carter determine what kind of reading instruction would best help Jacob. A number of strategies are useful for helping students read informational non-narrative texts with more engagement.

Teach Text Organization

Aside from teaching about the particular sections of information texts (e.g., table of contents, glossary, headings, appendices), teaching students about the different ways in which the content is organized can help them make more meaning of what they read.

Meyer (1985) pointed out the five most common ways in which informational non-narrative texts are organized:

- Description
- Sequence
- Comparison and contrast
- Cause and effect
- Problem solution

Providing students with examples of these formats, as well as helping them identify how the content of their own informational texts is organized, can better help them follow the logic and flow of what they are reading.

Use Text Maps

Specific instruction about text features helps students figure out what details are important in non-narrative informational text (Harvey & Goudvis, 2007). Text maps (Spencer, 2003) use the organizational features of a text to guide students as they read it. The teacher provides students with prompts based on text features to help them make sense of these signposts. Referring explicitly to a text's features, text maps help students preview a text, guide their reading, and then review the text in a way that further develops their understanding of it (see Figure 7.1).

Set Authentic Purposes for Reading

Reading to gain information is most powerful for students when they have authentic reasons to seek knowledge. After consulting with Jacob, Ms. Carter helped him identify specific things he wanted to find out from reading information texts: Why do some planets have moons? Where do comets come from? Why does Saturn have rings around it? What happens if a satellite breaks free from Earth's orbit, and how does that affect the Earth and the universe? Who decides what is defined as a "planet" and other parts of the universe (e.g., the changing status of Pluto such that it is no longer considered a planet)? Now Jacob read through the texts strategically and critically, rather than haphazardly or always linearly, to support his learning.

FIGURE 7.1. Text Map Template

Text Feature to Examine	What It Makes Me Think I Will Read About in This Text
Title:	
Pictures and captions:	
Important vocabulary words (usually in **boldface**):	
Headings and subheadings:	
Graphs and charts:	

Similarly, capitalizing on Jacob's inquisitive and gregarious personality, Ms. Carter positioned him as the expert on outer space. Charging Jacob with the responsibility of sharing his knowledge about the topic with the rest of the class or with an audience beyond the classroom brought greater focus to his reading and helped him think about the usefulness of each text he reads.

Build on Students' Use of Other Informational Media

Students are engaged in rich literacy practices with a variety of informational media that do not normally fit into the traditional reading curriculum, but their proficiency and enthusiasm in those practices are not to be discounted. Teachers can build tremendous momentum and interest in informational non-narrative texts if they recognize and utilize some of those practices. Students like Jacob already have a number of strategies at their disposal by virtue of

---

WORKING WITH ENGLISH LANGUAGE LEARNERS

- Include texts written in students' native language and bilingual texts as you model text-using strategies.
- Provide students with opportunities to try text-using practices in informational books written in their native languages.
- Have students work in pairs or small groups with other students who are at various levels of English proficiency and interested in similar topics to continue developing their language skills around informational non-narrative texts written in English.
- Encourage students to share what they learned from reading informational non-narrative texts through written, artistic, oral, or dramatic media.
- Provide lots of informational non-narrative texts across a spectrum of readability levels in English, and encourage the reading of both simple and more challenging texts.

---

reading Internet websites, most of which are written as informational texts. Ms. Carter could also concentrate on the strategies Jacob applies to other media, teaching him how to recontextualize those practices within his reading of informational books and articles.

HOW THE TURN-AROUND IMPACTED JACOB

Ms. Carter turned around her reading instruction for informational texts, and she and Jacob prepared a Powerful Reading Plan (see Figure 7.2). Jacob became a much more effective text-user as he learned to read informational texts in more meaningful and powerful ways:

- He took more time exploring each book or magazine in the classroom library before deciding to take it back with him to his seat, asking himself how he could use it to help him gain the information he sought.
- He spent more time reading each text, and he read it strategically, using knowledge about text features and organization to find the places that helped him answer his most pressing questions.
- He shared his enthusiasm with classmates, making his reading more self-driven and powerful.

FIGURE 7.2. Powerful Reading Plan

(completed by student and teacher)

Date of plan: *March*

I, *Jacob Martin*, plan to grow my reading practices, and over the next month I am going to focus on:

> *Choosing texts for a good purpose and using the features of informational texts to find information I'm looking for and to learn new things.*

To reach this goal, I plan to:

1. *Ask myself what my purpose is for each informational text I read.*

2. *Use text maps to help me decide if a book will have the information I want.*

I, *Ms. Carter*, plan to help you grow your reading practices, and over the next month I am going to focus on:

> *Helping you become a skillful text-user with informational books.*

To help you reach this goal, I will:

1. *Guide you in identifying what knowledge you want to learn from informational texts.*

2. *Supply you with text maps and text organization tools and help you use them.*

3. *Point out when strategies are similar to ones you already use at home.*

4. *Point out my text-using strategies as I read aloud.*

5. *Provide opportunities to use the Internet and other media as informational texts.*

Date of reflection: *April*

Student reflection on the goal(s) above: *When I ask myself what my purpose is, it's easier to choose and read these books. I can find things that interest me now. I use the table of contents, index, and headings to help me find what I'm looking for.*

Teacher reflection on the goal(s) above: *Wow! Jacob's approach to reading informational texts has really turned around because I took the time to really study and pay attention to the genre and his interests. He pauses and reflects on his purpose for reading and then wisely selects texts to read based on his reflection. He has also learned a great deal about text features and uses them frequently in order to locate the information he seeks. Jacob is now reading in this genre in a smarter, more interested, and more committed way. I think he's ready to pick one of the topics he's interested in and teach us all about it.*

Teaching students like Jacob about actively positioning themselves as text-users enables them to take control of their reading. Paying close attention to the characteristics and functions of different genres, like informational non-narrative texts, allows students to make thoughtful decisions about what they read.

CONNECTIONS TO THE FIVE-PART FRAMEWORK

- *Code-breaking*: As students search for information, use this opportunity to help them decode new words and become more fluent when reading them.
- *Meaning-making*: Developing word lists of new vocabulary helps students to become more powerful meaning-makers and to practice making connections and disconnections as they attempt to make sense of the texts.
- *Text-analyzing*: Informational texts present a powerful opportunity to consider whose perspective is being privileged and whose voices are neglected. It is also helpful to pair informational books with blogs, fictional texts, news broadcasts, and so on to broaden the scope of an inquiry from multiple perspectives (e.g., who benefits from space exploration and who does not; social, political, ecological, and economic costs of space exploration; etc.).

CHAPTER 8

Text-Using Resources: Digital Texts

KYLA: CLICKING ALL OVER THE PLACE

Kyla, a third-grade girl, concentrated on the computer screen before her. She was looking up information on the Internet about a recent transit union strike in a nearby city as part of an assignment. Typing the union's name into the search engine had generated thousands of results. Kyla clicked on the first one, which brought up a webpage busy with articles, columns, charts, photographs, advertisements, and links to related websites. Kyla clicked on a photo of some protesters, which only took her to a larger version of it. She clicked back to the first site and then on the link "About Us." This time, she was directed to a site full of text, names, histories, and statistical graphs. Kyla furrowed her brow and returned to the first site again. She clicked on photos, icons, audio and video clips, words that turned a different color when she rolled the cursor over them, and even an advertisement for a local restaurant—all things that could be clicked on as she read. Each time, she tried to read the new page that had opened on the screen and clicked around the site to explore. What began as a brief online search turned into an hour-long scavenger hunt. When her teacher, Ms. Garcia, asked about her work and the information she had found, Kyla launched into an unfocused recitation of scattered details.

BECOMING TEXT-USERS IN A DIGITAL WORLD

Digital texts include websites, blogs, online discussion groups, and other forms of writing that are read primarily on computer monitors or electronic screens. What distinguishes digital texts from traditional paper texts are the multiple modes of communicating that accompany the words and are often integral for making meaning. Readers of digital texts must pay attention to images, font size and color, hypertext, pull-down menus, search boxes, audio and video clips, and advertisements displayed on the screen. Moreover, a single click on any of these features can open a whole new page of digital text and media for readers. Coiro (2003) states: "Web-based texts are typically nonlinear, interactive, and inclusive of multiple media forms. Each of these characteristics affords new opportunities while also presenting a range of challenges that require new thought processes for making meaning" (p. 459). Therefore, teaching students to use digital texts also means teaching them to be active in their learning processes—a challenge that is both exciting and sometimes overwhelming.

Many teachers now incorporate some form of digital texts into their classroom instruction, and as publishing companies increasingly put print materials online, some schools, universities, and local libraries are opting to procure electronic versions of materials instead of printed copies. The proliferation of these types of texts has also radically transformed the way students (and all people) read in their everyday lives. Digital texts are here to stay and need to be used in classroom instruction in order to equip our students, like Kyla, to become powerful users of them. The new technology standards set by the International Society for Technology in

---

BY THE END OF THIS CHAPTER, YOU WILL:

- Understand how reading digital texts can help students develop a variety of literacy practices necessary for the 21st century
- Understand the most common types of digital texts
- Think critically about using digital texts in your classroom
- Have specific tools to help you *learn about your students' use* of digital texts
- Have specific strategies to assist students in becoming effective users of digital texts

---

Education (ISTE) and the Partnership for 21st Century Skills (2007–2008) insist that schools must embrace technology to stay competitive in the global environment.

Regardless of whether digital texts are part of the official school curriculum, students are reading them on their own—often with intense engagement and, in many cases, more often and more willingly than printed texts. When students read digital texts, they continue to develop the code-breaking and meaning-making skills required to read conventional print material, and they simultaneously employ a number of other complex literacy practices, such as adapting to changing genres and engaging various modalities of learning (e.g., visual, kinesthetic, auditory). Such literacy flexibility is vital for an increasingly digital and globalized society, but it is largely neglected in school literacy curricula. This chapter discusses ways to turn around our pedagogies to use two types of digital texts—websites and blogs—to help grow powerful text-using practices for our students.

Navigating Websites

When I (Grace) was in elementary school, I had to do a big report on tigers that required using an encyclopedia for my research. I went to the library and searched the volumes until I found the Th–Ty volume. I paged through it alphabetically until I came to the word *tiger* and then read the two pages dedicated to tigers to gather information for my report. Today, when I type *tiger* into Google, I get directed to 34,700,000 websites packed with tons of information. Means of finding information have changed dramatically in my short lifetime, and the Internet has changed the way we think about accessing the world. Websites come in a variety of formats and from a variety of sources. While most sites are commercial (.com), sites that have governmental (.gov), organizational (.org), and educational (.edu) addresses may be particularly useful for academic purposes. Watts-Taffe and Gwinn (2007) point out that the phrase "navigating texts" is especially appropriate for readers of websites, since so much of what one "reads" isn't bound to a single page or screenview. The ability to search for worthwhile information online and use websites is a crucial skill, and teaching it needs thoughtful consideration and powerful strategies.

Reading and Responding to Blogs

Blogs (an abbreviation of *web logs*) are a popular form of digital text in abundance on the Internet. Blogs focus on a particular topic or two from an "insider's perspective," usually a single author or a group of people sharing a similar outlook on the matter. Because of this kind of authorship, readers need to clearly know their purpose for reading a blog, as well as the purpose of the author(s).

Blogs have a unique format and set of features that emphasize issues of organization and audience while reading. Blogs are organized chronologically, with the date posted on each entry and usually a list of archived entries along one of the margins. Most entries also include a list of keywords or labels for readers to click on to find other related entries. Blogs also offer links and places for readers to respond to the entries. Readers can immediately respond to content by adding comments at the bottom of each entry they read, thus highlighting the aspect of text-using that requires "being able to respond to texts in a variety of ways" (Rush, 2004, p. 38). This medium is also becoming a powerful tool for classroom instruction and impacts the way we think about text-using.

THINKING CRITICALLY ABOUT CLASSROOM PRACTICE: WHAT IS YOUR APPROACH TO DIGITAL TEXTS?

Many teachers believe that digital texts deserve a place in their reading instruction, but they're not quite sure what to do with them, and they don't want to squelch the enthusiasm that students like Kyla show for reading by telling them they can't use digital texts. A

TEACHER EXERCISE:
THINKING ABOUT YOUR OWN PRACTICES WITH DIGITAL TEXTS

Think of a topic that you are interested in.

1. Type this keyword into a search engine (like Google or Yahoo).
2. How many hits did you get?
3. What types of sites does the search engine direct you to?

Pick one website to go to from this list.

1. What do you notice about this site?
2. How is it laid out?
3. Where does your eye go first?
4. What information does it contain?
5. Where are the links?
6. Who is it created/sponsored by?
7. What is the date of this site or the dates of its most recent entries?
8. How long do you spend on this site before you move to another one?
9. When you are on this site, do you stay in one place or jump around?
10. What perspective(s) is (are) the content written from?
11. What other forms of media are included?
12. Based on your experience, what might be some helpful practices for navigating digital texts?

---

first step toward helping students to productively use these texts is to turn a critical eye on your own teaching practices:

- Do I provide explicit instruction about the various genres and purposes of texts that are available online?
- Do I incorporate enough time in my classroom instruction for students to read digital texts on a regular basis?
- Do I allow students to read only the digital texts I assign them, or do I teach and encourage them to make meaningful selections about the digital texts they read?
- Do I leave students alone to read digital texts because I view it as something mostly extracurricular, or do I confer with them individually and in small groups to guide their reading of digital texts?
- Do I encourage students to read digital texts representing multiple perspectives on the same topic to foster text analysis?

GETTING TO KNOW STUDENTS WELL: HOW DO THEY USE DIGITAL TEXTS?

While thinking critically about teaching practices is a necessary step for transforming reading instruction, teachers also need to make sure that instruction is appropriate. To help students like Kyla be better text-users of digital texts, first we need to understand how Kyla is currently using these texts. Many of these steps are similar to text-using of other texts, but with more of a focus on the unique features of digital texts.

Surveying Technology Use

A technology-using survey (see Figure 8.1) is a powerful way to get to know a student's practices with computer-based technology in both classroom endeavors and personal life.

Assessing Knowledge of Digital Text Structure

It is one thing to know about Kyla's text usage, but it is another to understand how she perceives the text structures of digital texts. Coiro and Dobler (2007) found that online reading comprehension shared a number of similarities with offline reading—but also included a number of important differences. Some of these differences revolved around the purpose of the text (why are you accessing digital text?), the reading task itself (what strategies do you need?), and the context of the text itself. Understanding a student's knowledge of the structure of digital text is an important starting point in developing effective instruction. In a conversation with a student, you can ask the following questions:

FIGURE 8.1. Technology-Using Survey

At school:

- What kinds of digital texts do you use at school?
- Why do you use these types of texts at school?
- When you are looking for information on the computer, what do you do first?
- How much time in school would you say that you use digital texts?

FIGURE 8.1. *continued*

At home:

1. Rank the technology devices you use most often.
    (1 = most and 5 = least)

    _____ Cell phone
    _____ Computer
    _____ Gaming systems (Playstation, Wii, X-box)
    _____ Handheld
    _____ Other_____

2. On average, about how much time *per day* do you spend using computer-based technology?

    _____ Little or no time
    _____ 15–30 minutes
    _____ 30–60 minutes
    _____ 1–3 hours
    _____ More than 3 hours

3. If you use technology, *check* your *top five* reasons *why*.

    _____ E-mailing friends or family
    _____ Text-messaging friends or family
    _____ School assignments
    _____ Online gaming
    _____ Social networking
    _____ Surfing the Internet
    _____ Watching videos
    _____ Making/editing videos
    _____ Downloading/listening to music
    _____ Making/editing music
    _____ Participating in a fan site
    _____ Using handheld, television-based, or computer-based video games
    _____ Blogging
    _____ Other _____

4. How would you rate your overall comfort level with computer-based technology?

    _____ Expert
    _____ Very comfortable
    _____ Moderately comfortable
    _____ Not very comfortable
    _____ Uncomfortable

- What are some common structures of websites?
    Hyperlinks
    Icons
    Interactive multimedia
    More prominent links
    Homepage vs. linked pages

- How do you find information on the Internet?
    What search engines do you use?
    What is a browser tool bar and what is it used for?
    How are websites arranged when you use a search engine?
    How is text constructed (organizational and structural features such as headings, index, boldface, italicized, hypertexts, etc.)?

When Ms. Garcia sat with Kyla to discuss Kyla's use of text structures, she discovered that Kyla was very comfortable using the Internet and used it frequently at home. She knew how to use a search engine but did not know how websites were organized once she got results. Also, while she had a good understanding of how to navigate once in a website by using links and multimedia options, she often spent more time just clicking back and forth without knowing how to use these features with a purpose. Based on this information, Ms. Garcia worked with Kyla to develop the Powerful Reading Plan shown in Figure 8.2.

WHAT TEACHERS CAN DO: TURN-AROUND STRATEGIES TO ENHANCE DIGITAL-TEXT USE

It is imperative that teachers use digital texts alongside conventional print texts in their instruction. Alternating digital texts with paper texts in read-alouds, shared and choral reading, mini-lesson demonstrations, and mentor texts is a powerful way to promote flexible reading practices.

Setting Purposes for Reading

All students need to set purposes for reading any text, but when you unleash them into a world of about 200,000,000 websites

FIGURE 8.2. Powerful Reading Plan

(completed by student and teacher)

Date of plan: *September*

I, *Kyla Howard*, plan to grow my reading practices, and over the next month I am going to focus on:

> *Deciding on a purpose for reading texts online and learning to locate important information for my plan once on a website.*

To reach this goal, I plan to:

1. *Set purposes for reading and stick to them, noticing when I get distracted.*

2. *Skim, scan, and just read information that seems like it fits with my plan.*

3. *Predict and infer what supporting text or media may be linked to the text.*

I, *Ms. Garcia*, plan to help you grow your reading practices, and over the next month I am going to focus on:

> *Providing explicit instruction about reading digital texts to the whole class and incorporating more digital texts into my reading instruction.*

To help you reach this goal, I will:

1. *Use digital texts alongside printed texts during my mini-lessons and read-alouds.*

2. *Use think-alouds to model how I navigate digital texts with a purpose.*

3. *Give you more time to read digital texts during independent reading time.*

Date of reflection: *November*

Student reflections on the goal(s) above: *I used to get lost when I was reading. Now I know how to stop and think about what to click on. I like doing work on the Internet.*

Teacher reflections on the goal(s) above: *Kyla's work with digital texts has improved tremendously. She carefully articulates and reviews her purpose for reading online whenever she encounters a website full of text and multimedia features. She also previews each site by skimming and scanning what's on it to decide what's most helpful for her purpose. Kyla has a great knowledge base about using digital texts already, and I will continue to build on that as I teach the whole class and work with her.*

per topic, it is even more important for students to set clear purposes for using websites and blogs. For example, when Kyla went to the Internet to look up the transit strike, she got distracted by the sidebars, videos, and multimedia and lost track of what she was originally pursuing. Although some of the fun with the Internet is discovering things you were not planning to find, if we want our students to become savvy users of this type of text, we also need to give them tools to help rein them in when they stray. By using a flowchart similar to the one shown in Figure 8.3, students can keep track of the websites they visit and make sure those sites help them address the purpose they set for reading.

Skimming and Scanning Texts for Information

Watts-Taffe and Gwinn (2007) asserts that "the volume of text available on the Internet requires readers to engage more fully in

FIGURE 8.3. Setting a Purpose

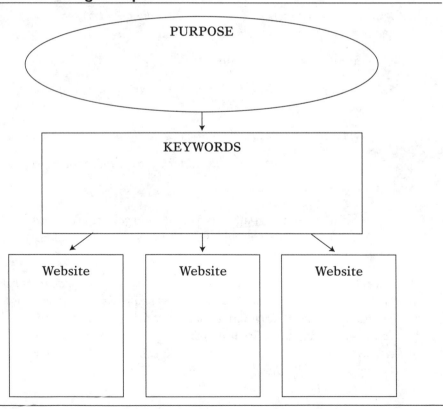

skimming, scanning, and selective reading than they have in the past" (p. 63). Since multiple kinds of related texts are just a click or scroll away, readers need to make smart decisions about what content will be most useful for their reading goals. Using a skimming and scanning graphic organizer will help students become more effective information gatherers from digital texts (see Figure 8.4). By noting only the most important information from each site, students can quickly decide whether a website is helpful for their reading purposes and whether it is worth reading.

Teaching Text Organization

When we teach text organization to students, we need to use think-alouds to explicitly acknowledge, name, and model the multiple literacies one employs while reading digital texts. When teachers expand how they talk about reading in their classrooms, they help students understand how to apply many of their print-reading skills to their reading of websites and blogs; they also help students understand that literacy practices beyond those that are traditionally valued in school curricula are necessary for reading in all areas of life (Siegel, Kontovourki, Schmier, & Enriquez, 2008). In your think-alouds, you can model how you address questions such as the following:

FIGURE 8.4. Skimming and Scanning Graphic Organizer

Website	Important Information	Helpful?	
		Yes	No

WORKING WITH ENGLISH LANGUAGE LEARNERS

- Encourage students to search for useful sites in their native languages.
- Spend equal time discussing the information provided through both the print and the other media on the site.
- Encourage students to create digital texts—such as digital stories, short films, blogs, podcasts, and so on—to explore issues that may be important to them (e.g., family histories, policies on language use in the United States, immigration experiences, living in two-language worlds, etc.).

- Where is the main text located on a website/blog?
- Is there a site map or a list of major links? Minor links? Where is this located?
- Does this site have:

Links?	Videos?
Photos?	Advertisements?

Thinking Critically About Using Websites and Blogs

Just as we want our students to think critically about texts that we use in the classroom, we also want students to be critical consumers of digital texts. The amount of information available on the Internet guarantees that students will come across sites that are highly controversial or that promote information that is simply wrong (for example, sites promoting the idea that the Holocaust never happened). Like all published texts, digital texts are limited by their authors' perspectives and purposes and should be considered within a social and temporal context. For example, students should know how to locate the date the text was last updated and the sources of the content in order to decide whether the site or blog is relevant to their inquiries and to assess the trustworthiness of the site, its author(s), and the content.

HOW THE TURN-AROUND IMPACTED KYLA

Kyla sat in the computer lab the following week to continue her reading about the union strike. Ms. Garcia had taught several mini-lessons that specifically addressed practices for using digital texts.

Kyla had become less distracted in her reading of digital texts and was continuing to grow as a powerful user of them:

1. Kyla went back to the first site she found after typing the union's name into the search engine.
2. Consulting the chart she had completed, she reminded herself that her purpose was to find out what rights the union was fighting for (refer to Figure 8.3).
3. She saw a few paragraphs toward the bottom of the site on employment rights, as well as some links within those paragraphs that could provide her with more information.
4. She knew that this text and the related links would be useful for her research, so she focused on reading those—but she first took note of those pages on her graphic organizer to keep track of her work (refer to Figure 8.4).
5. Kyla presented this information to the class as the students decided on ways they could support the city workers in their communities.

CONNECTIONS TO THE FIVE-PART FRAMEWORK

- *Code-breaking*: Students are often highly motivated to read digital texts, creating optimum conditions for decoding unfamiliar words.
- *Meaning-making*: Digital texts usually contain links to other digital texts that further define words or explain information that students can use to help them understand the content of a site.
- *Text-analyzing*: Students can use the information about who created the site or published information on it to critically question what they find online. They can also purposefully search for sites that provide different perspectives on a topic.
- *Identity-constructing*: As students gain more confidence and purpose in their digital-text use in school, they will begin to construct stronger identities as readers of digital texts—an identity that can be used to strengthen their overall perceptions of themselves as readers.

Part V

TEXT-ANALYZING

A Five-Part Framework for Powerful Reading

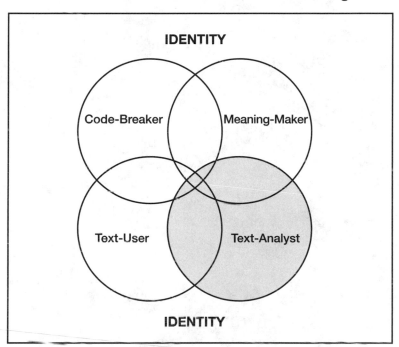

CHAPTER 9

Text Analysis: Deconstructing and Reconstructing Texts

MERCEDES: SHUTTING DOWN AND ACTING OUT

Lashell came running out of the girls' bathroom: "Ms. Reilly, Ms. Reilly, Mercedes is fighting again." Ms. Reilly stepped into the bathroom to see an all-too-familiar scene and escorted Mercedes to her spot at the back of the room—again! Since Mercedes had entered this fifth-grade class a month ago, she had caused many sleepless nights for her teacher. Although Mercedes had a decent command of English, she was reluctant to complete any assignments in anything other than her native Spanish, and she had a difficult time positively interacting with others in class. It seemed that Mercedes spent more time inside the in-school suspension room than in her own classroom. Mercedes spent most of the 75-minute language arts block with her head on her desk, rarely participating in any classroom activities. Ms. Reilly had not spent enough time with Mercedes to know whether it was her trouble with English, trouble with classmates, or trouble with reading that caused her to shut down each day. Ms. Reilly was frustrated and was not sure how to reach Mercedes. She knew that her own inability to speak to Mercedes in Spanish, the large number of students she had in her third-period English class, and her lack of experience as a new teacher all erected barriers to finding ways to reach Mercedes. However, Ms. Reilly was determined not to let any of her students fall through the cracks and was committed to reaching Mercedes.

THINKING CRITICALLY ABOUT CLASSROOM PRACTICE: HOW DO YOU SUPPORT TEXT ANALYSIS?

Ms. Reilly was frustrated by Mercedes's lack of participation and concerned about the seeming lack of motivation and engagement of several other students. Ms. Reilly had diligently worked with students all year on decoding multisyllabic words, using context to determine word meanings, developing fluency, and reading with expression. She taught students how to use vocabulary and comprehension strategies to make meaning of the texts they were reading and how to navigate genres such as informational texts, multiple genres of fiction, and websites. But she had not adequately prepared her students to be text-analysts. Text-analysts think critically about literacy as a social practice: how we read, what we read, and how we consider power and positioning in texts.

BY THE END OF THIS CHAPTER, YOU WILL:

- Understand why it is important for students to be text-analysts
- Understand how teachers can use text deconstruction and reconstruction to connect with *all* students
- Identify classroom strategies to use for teaching text analysis
- Realize how text deconstruction and reconstruction can lead to more powerful reading practices for students

> **TEACHER EXERCISE:**
> **THINKING ABOUT YOUR INSTRUCTIONAL PRACTICES**
>
> - Think about your reading instruction. Approximately how much time do you spend on:
>
>   > Code-breaking activities?
>   > Meaning-making activities?
>   > Text-using activities?
>   > Text-analysis activities?
>
> - Is there one area that you spend significantly more time with? Less time?
> - Do your instructional practices take into account helping students read both the word and the world around them?
> - Do you have readers who are shutting down or acting out? Could changing your instruction alter this behavior?

From her reading as part of a teacher study group, Ms. Reilly began to realize how social dynamics can affect a literacy classroom and to consider her students' overall perspectives of the world around them. She wanted to encourage her students to be critical readers of the *word* and readers of the *world* (Freire, 1970), while simultaneously reaching out to Mercedes and supporting better social relations in her classroom. First she needed to consider what she did and didn't do in her classroom around text analysis. With Ms. Reilly, think about your own answers to the following questions:

- Do I foster opportunities for students to hear multiple voices in a text, to question the author, and to critique a text?
- Do I give students the opportunity to talk with one another through the reading process so that they can see how others perceive issues raised in texts?
- Do I open up the classroom as a safe place for students to talk about social issues important to them?
- Do I demonstrate the *deconstructing* of texts by identifying themes relating to sexism, racism, classism, ableism, heterosexism, and other oppressive practices that work to maintain the status quo in our society?

- Do I demonstrate the *reconstructing* of texts by highlighting my conscious choice of words in oral and written language to work toward social action and justice?
- Do I use teachable moments throughout the day to explore issues of power, positioning, and perspective in text and in the classroom (e.g., Jones, 2006)?
- Do I help students see the link between the textual work that we do and the broader world around them?

WHAT IS TEXT DECONSTRUCTION AND RECONSTRUCTION?

After Ms. Reilly had critically considered her classroom practices, she realized she wasn't doing anything to support her students in becoming text-analysts. Furthermore, she felt that encouraging textual and social critique could motivate Mercedes and other students to participate in language arts in a way that her decoding and meaning-making lessons had not. She tried to turn around her students' engagement by first turning herself around. Ms. Reilly began to turn around her reading pedagogies by stepping into new territory around text deconstruction and reconstruction, rooted in critical literacy practices. Students are provided with the tools to read and critique messages in texts, to question whose knowledge is being privileged, and to confront what texts say about particular groups of people and particular ways of living.

Text Deconstruction

Deconstruction literally means "to take something apart." An important lesson for all readers to learn, especially those who are marginalized by texts, is that all texts are *constructed*, or created, by someone. Therefore, all texts can be *de*constructed, or taken apart to better understand the perspectives informing them. Ms. Reilly wanted to start with a text that highlighted multiple perspectives in order to support early lessons she had taught on considering perspective and power. She chose *Seedfolks* (Fleishman, 1997), a book about an urban community garden with each chapter told from a different character's perspective about how the garden has impacted his or her life. Ms. Reilly hoped the diversity of perspectives and relevance of the stories would reach different students—especially

Mercedes. As Ms. Reilly read aloud, she also talked about her analyses of perspective and power in different chapters, and she kept a chart of questions for the students to consider:

- Why do some people have power over the garden and others do not?
- Whose voices are given power? Whose voices are silenced?
- Why do you think the author chose to represent these specific voices as well as different perspectives?

Ms. Reilly also asked her students to make connections and disconnections with the characters and social situations they read about (see Chapter 5). As she read aloud, Ms. Reilly noticed that Mercedes slowly began paying attention—especially when she got to the chapter about Maricela, a 16-year-old pregnant girl from Mexico. Later that day, when students were writing about the book, she noticed that Mercedes wrote constantly until the bell rang. After asking Mercedes if she could read her journal entry, Ms. Reilly learned that Mercedes was experiencing similar isolation for being Mexican, as most people in her neighborhood were from Guatemala or Puerto Rico. Mercedes alluded to the tension within the Spanish-speaking community and wrote that she hated it when others lumped her together with other groups of Spanish speakers. She also wrote about feeling powerless and ignored at home because her older sister had just had a baby.

Ms. Reilly's careful selection of text (one that highlighted multiple perspectives, diverse experiences, and a character with a similar heritage as her most marginalized student, Mercedes) and her pointed questions around issues of power and perspective helped to open up a space of engagement and social critique.

Text Reconstruction

Ms. Reilly slowly saw some changes in student engagement as she raised her expectations for students as text-analysts, but she realized that she needed to go beyond deconstruction. She wanted to give students opportunities to use their insights about power, positioning, and perspective in texts to create new ways of thinking about themselves, texts they read, and their larger world. Ms. Reilly decided that she needed to take this next step and help students move from a critical reading of texts (deconstruction) to creating

new texts that were more socially just or at least offered important counterstories to those in mainstream books (reconstruction).
In doing this, Ms. Reilly believed some of her least engaged students (including Mercedes) would begin to reconstruct their reading identities in more productive ways.

One opportunity arose when a fight broke out in the cafeteria,
which led the principal to create strict guidelines for cafeteria behavior. Ms. Reilly's students were outraged, and she used their motivation and passion to engage in reconstruction. The next day, she
asked students to think about the work they had been doing as text-
analysts and to recreate the cafeteria scene emphasizing perspective and power. She asked students to write from the perspective
of the principal, the teacher involved, the students involved, and
the students who were bystanders. The students diligently wrote
and reconstructed the events from different perspectives. They read
their pieces to the class and discussed various perspectives. After
having a heated debate about whether or not students have power
in schools, they decided to create a lunchtime Bill of Rights to ap-
peal to the principal to reconsider his use of power to create more
stringent rules for all students.

WHAT TEACHERS CAN DO: TURN-AROUND STRATEGIES TO PROMOTE TEXT ANALYSIS

Ms. Reilly knew that text deconstruction and reconstruction
should be occurring throughout her schoolday and schoolyear,
not just in isolated lessons or social events. She turned to many
other ideas that could be infused into her classroom throughout
the schoolyear.

Text Deconstruction

Book Selection and Probing Questions. There are many great
books that purposefully emphasize multiple perspectives and provide an entry point to text deconstruction (see the Appendix). However, *all* texts should be questioned around issues of who exercises
power, whose voices are prominent and whose are marginalized or
excluded, and why a text is written from a certain perspective. For
example, students could explore the following questions:

- Why did the author choose to represent a certain character as a boy or a girl? Would it matter if the story were told from a different gender perspective?
- Why did the author choose to set his or her story in a certain social-class location? How would the story have changed if it were set in a different community?
- What characters do not have a prominent voice in the story? Why do you think the author chose to highlight certain characters but not others? How would the story change from a different point of view?
- Why did the author decide to make the characters of a certain racial background?

This kind of critical analysis is imperative, as it develops students' habits of mind and promotes the notion that texts are always grounded in ideology and situated in social and political contexts; therefore, every text should be challenged and questioned.

Critical Reading Journal and "Question the Author." By keeping a critical reading journal, students can write in response to the deconstruction process. For example, students can create double-entry journal pages where they react to different characters, settings, and social issues in books and other texts. A "question the author" section can be used to question why the author made certain choices in creating the text. This journal can be a reaction to books read in class, books read independently, as well as other texts such as movies, television shows, or events that occur in the students' lives.

Critical Reader's Theater. Reader's Theater is a wonderful way to get students to literally hear multiple perspectives in a text. For example, in *George vs. George: The American Revolution as Seen from Both Sides* (Schanzer, 2004), students can work in groups to create a script for both King George and George Washington. By probing different and conflicting points of view—especially those not heard from often—students can see how power and perspective can silence various parts of every story and impact how we interpret history.

Text Reconstruction

Diary Entries. One powerful reconstruction activity is to write diary entries from an excluded or marginalized perspective. For example, after reading the traditional account of Columbus's landing in the New World and then the book *Encounter* (Yolen, 1992), which retells this familiar narrative from a different perspective, students can write a diary entry of the first encounter through the eyes of a young Taino boy. This activity can create a wonderful entry point to discussions about marginalized peoples and perspectives and can begin to give voice to those who have not historically had one in mainstream texts.

Rewriting Familiar Stories. Another successful writing activity is to recreate a story for the purpose of challenging stereotypes in the text. For example, students can choose a story like Cinderella and recreate it through writing to challenge the following:

- The sexist stereotype of a woman in need of rescuing by a man
- The images of "beauty" as represented by Cinderella and "lack of beauty" as represented by the stepsisters and stepmother
- The positioning of "poor" people as needing to be rescued by someone with great wealth
- The racialized representation in the book
- The assumption that men and women (not same-sex partners) are the assumed "couple" in this and other books

Again, through writing students can take what they learned about power, positioning, and perspective in deconstruction and recreate a new story.

HOW THE TURN-AROUND IMPACTED MERCEDES

Reading *Seedfolks* and talking with the students about deconstruction and reconstruction started getting Mercedes' attention, and Ms. Reilly found that this avenue was a powerful way to connect with this student. Using a text-analysis approach, Ms. Reilly and Mercedes came up with a Powerful Reading Plan to get her engaged in reading and help her develop more positive relationships with other students (see Figure 9.1).

Three weeks later, Lashell hurried out of the bathroom and commented breathlessly, "Ms. Reilly, she's at it again." Overall,

FIGURE 9.1. Powerful Reading Plan

(completed by student and teacher)

Date of plan: *April*

I, *Mercedes Villanueva*, plan to grow my reading practices, and over the next month I am going to focus on:

> *Noticing how some people's perspectives are important in books and other people's are not—or they're not included.*

To reach this goal, I plan to:

1. *Start a critical reading journal and think about perspectives as I read different texts.*

2. *Think about power and perspective with other texts and situations, like in my music and on the Disney channel.*

3. *Keep a personal journal to write about my feelings about my sister, my community, my family, and places where I feel powerless and powerful.*

I, *Ms. Reilly*, plan to help you grow your reading practices, and over the next month I am going to focus on:

> *Paying attention to different perspectives in texts and social situations at school and thinking about how people and authors use their power to make the world better or to keep the world like it is.*

To help you reach this goal, I will:

1. *Help you find books that present different points of view.*

2. *Have conferences with you about issues of power, positioning, and perspective in your reading.*

3. *Help you keep a "question the author" part of your critical reading journal.*

Date of reflection: *May*

Student reflection on the goal(s) above: *I started keeping a double-entry journal to think about the different points of views of characters. This taught me that everyone has a different perspective, although sometimes certain perspectives have more power. I try to think about this when I get angry at people in my class—that they have a perspective, too.*

Teacher reflection on the goal(s) above: *Mercedes has become a more engaged reader and thinker. By keeping her journal and considering multiple points of view, power, and how authors (and people in real life) position others, she has become a more critical reader, thinker, and actor in her own situations.*

WORKING WITH ENGLISH LANGUAGE LEARNERS

- Provide texts that represent immigration experiences that are rarely in school books. This perpetual "exclusion" of various immigration experiences and immigrants themselves is a ripe place to start for critically reading texts in schools.
- Explore how reconstructing texts in bilingual and multilingual ways can challenge the English-only culture in the United States while inspiring English language learners to reposition themselves and their languages as valuable.
- Become aware of how many students are frustrated by the ways they are misidentified by people making assumptions about their heritage based on the color of their skin or the language they speak. These social practices can be disrupted by students speaking out about the issue and engaging in a social action project to educate fellow students, teachers, and people in the larger community.

Mercedes had been making much progress in her classroom engagement and social relations, but there was still work to do.

Ms. Reilly only had to poke her head into the bathroom before Mercedes hung her head and came out. Instead of calling the principal, however, Ms. Reilly sat Mercedes and her sparring partner down at the back of the class and asked them to write and/or draw what the disagreement was about from each other's point of view. This provided time for them to cool off and also to think about different sides of the issue and how they were each using their power in the situation to position the other. Ms. Reilly was pleased that her instructional focus on being critical seemed to be facilitating more productive social relations, and she felt that her work in creating critically literate citizens was starting to pay off.

CONNECTIONS TO THE FIVE-PART FRAMEWORK

- *Meaning-making*: Emphasizing the connections and disconnections students make with texts can help them consider questions of power, privilege, and perspective.
- *Text-using*: Modeling how to deconstruct and reconstruct different genres of text, especially informational texts that too often seem to speak with ultimate authority on a matter, is a great way to deepen students' work as text-users and text-analysts.
- *Identity-constructing*: Many students who are not motivated by more traditional work in reading often become highly motivated and enthusiastic when invited to engage as critical readers of texts and of their world. This repositioning of themselves in relation to reading is an important turn-around for their reading success.

Text-Analyzing Resources: Reading for Social Justice

EDDIE: CHECKING OUT OF READING AND SCHOOL

Eddie, a polite, 7-year-old Latino boy, had moved to a new neighborhood in the city over the winter vacation and entered Ms. Whitlow's second-grade class in January. He seemed to be doing fine in reading for the first few weeks, but then Ms. Whitlow began noticing him dawdling during reading workshop and growing distracted during read-aloud time. She also noticed that he was withdrawing from the classmates who had befriended him when he first joined the class. One day, Ms. Whitlow sat down with Eddie to check in with him about his reading. Using books that were both appropriate and instructional for his reading level, she listened to him read and answer basic comprehension questions, which he did rather mechanically but mostly correctly. Unsure about what to do with Eddie, she thanked him for his time and moved to talk with another student. Ten minutes later, Eddie was still staring distractedly at the same page.

Eddie was not necessarily a poor reader, but he was also not the kind of reader who got excited about reading. Additionally, reading did not seem as important to him as whatever else was going on in his life, especially with his friends. If Eddie were to continue in this way, over the next few years he could grow uninterested in reading or resistant to it, ultimately slowing down his reading development, which would prevent him from keeping up with his classmates and potentially put him at risk of being labeled a "struggling reader." Eddie needed not just any reason to keep reading; he needed one that showed him how powerful texts can be and how they can even make change in the world.

READING FOR SOCIAL JUSTICE

I (Grace) remember, as a college student, being exhilarated in my freshman seminar class by an ongoing discussion about the contributions of 20th-century American playwrights. The pace was fast and animated, the conversation so sophisticated, and I kept wondering, "How can I enter this? What can I contribute? What business do I have even trying? What if I make a fool out of myself?" And so I followed the talk, scribbled page after page of notes, and sat in awe of my classmates and professor, feeling like a helpless bystander.

BY THE END OF THIS CHAPTER, YOU WILL:

- Understand what it means to engage in reading for social justice
- Understand why reading for social justice is important for helping students become text-analysts
- Think critically about your own reading instruction around social justice issues
- Have specific tools to help you *learn about social injustices in students' lives* in order to create meaningful instruction
- Have specific suggestions for guiding students as they read toward goals of social justice

Trying to help children grow and develop into thoughtful citizens can be just like my overwhelming experience in that freshman seminar class. As teachers, we watch in awe at how quickly our students learn and how complex the world becomes for them. And sometimes, despite our best efforts to teach them, we, too, can feel like helpless bystanders, wondering if there's a way we can contribute something more significant to their lives. Ms. Whitlow felt like this about Eddie.

Many teachers enter the profession to make a meaningful difference in the lives of students. They believe that equipping children with the knowledge and skills needed as adults is an important contribution to society and future generations. And while that's true, if students aren't also learning to apply those skills to confront injustices around them, what kind of social contribution are teachers preparing them to make? If all teachers are doing is passing on functional skills, are students also being prepared only to assume roles as helpless bystanders, without a real voice in matters of the world?

Reading for social justice can help you turn around your pedagogy to make sure you are teaching students how to make their voices heard. You can do this by teaching students to analyze texts through a critical lens while reading.

When teachers and students read for social justice, they can begin questioning injustices and issues of oppression. When teachers help students read for social justice, they not only make a meaningful difference in the lives of students, they also teach students that they, too, can use literacy as a powerful tool to make a difference in their own lives. Reading takes on an active role in students' lives, not just for school, for tests, for gaining information, or for pleasure, but for transforming and rewriting experiences in the world.

TEACHER EXERCISE: THINKING ABOUT
YOUR OWN EXPERIENCE WITH READING FOR SOCIAL JUSTICE

1. Make a list of the social injustices in the world that you worry about in your own life.
2. Now make a list of the books you read as a child. Did any of them help you begin to think more deeply about those issues? If so, how?
3. Think about how the kinds of reading you do now help you explore and address the injustices that matter to you.

THINKING CRITICALLY ABOUT CLASSROOM PRACTICE: WHAT ROLE DOES SOCIAL JUSTICE PLAY IN READING INSTRUCTION?

Ms. Whitlow worked hard to make sure her students were well equipped with the reading skills they need to gain future opportunities. She was of two minds about Eddie: (1) perplexed and curious when he did not respond to reading the way other students did and (2) tired, feeling the thousands of other pressures of her job and thinking about asking someone to run a battery of tests on Eddie. Fortunately for Eddie, she let her first reaction guide her next steps, and she began looking more critically at her own instruction and classroom practices.

Reread the Representations in Classroom Texts

Ms. Whitlow first surveyed the texts and materials she regularly used when teaching reading. She discovered that her classroom library was filled with picture books and beginning chapter books that she had loved as a child. She also used many of her favorites when reading aloud to students or demonstrating points about reading or writing. A lot of the books in Ms. Whitlow's classroom library projected images of children who romped around their tree-lined neighborhoods, played with their puppies, went to a single-family home to eat a hearty dinner, and got tucked into bed with a goodnight kiss from their married mother and father. A lot of the classroom books were also about girls who wore lots of pink clothes and took dance lessons. Then Ms. Whitlow looked around her classroom and noticed that they were boys and girls from diverse ethnic and socioeconomic backgrounds. Some of them had single parents; some lived with foster parents or with siblings, parents, cousins, aunts, uncles, and grandparents in small apartments; and some lived in what some might call "rough" neighborhoods. Reading texts about puppies and pink dresses might have entertained her students, but it also ignored the real experiences of each student's life.

Consider Instructional Delivery

Sometimes teachers have restricted choices for reading materials in schools, but we recommend a careful rethinking about how required reading materials are used. The classroom structures and instructional approaches teachers use impact how students interpret the purposes and goals of reading. Reflecting on her daily activities with students, Ms. Whitlow realized that she had structured their reading time to be mostly silent and isolated. Such isolation is characteristic of many contemporary reading programs (Wilson & Laman, 2007), but it is far from what is promoted by many literacy researchers and experts (Allington, 2005; Calkins, 2001; Taberski, 2000). Rarely did Ms. Whitlow's students get to share their ideas or questions about what they were reading with one another. She was the only person to engage them in that kind of dialogue, and such conversations were focused on questions she posed to the student about decoding, vocabulary, or basic meaning-making. If she wanted students to view reading as an inspirational and important instrument for making change, Ms. Whitlow knew she needed to provide daily opportunities for them to read for social justice.

Assess the Scope of Curriculum

In an era of high-stakes testing, it's easy for teachers to get caught up in the official school curriculum, since that is what they will be officially held accountable for teaching. But lots of people, including teachers, also hold schools accountable for ensuring that students become active, productive citizens in our country's democracy. After taking a long, hard look at her teaching, Ms. Whitlow admitted she clung to the "safety" and "comfort" of the official curriculum. But being safe and comfortable also sent the message to students to accept the status quo. Teaching her students why literacy mattered meant teaching them all of its possibilities in their lives. Along with Ms. Whitlow, think about the following questions related to classroom practice:

- Do I select texts that are grounded in students' real-life experiences, interests, and concerns to read aloud with them?
- Does my classroom library represent a number of perspectives, lifestyles, cultures, and geographic locations in the texts, or do they mostly depict mainstream representations of people and experiences?
- Do I restrict students' reading time to quiet, individual activities, or do I promote work in partnerships and small

groups so students can benefit from the perspectives of others?

- When I talk with students about what they are reading, do I limit those conversations to discussions about the text, or do I extend them to help students consider what the text says about the world?
- Do I teach reading for its own sake, or do I help students see how reading can be used to explore many perspectives and social injustices?
- Do I work beyond curriculum mandates by helping students use their reading and writing skills to address real problems in their lives and communities?

GETTING TO KNOW STUDENTS WELL: WHAT ARE THEIR CONCERNS?

Ms. Whitlow needed to reassess what she knew about Eddie in order to shift his perception of reading. She had several options for doing this, ranging from quick observations that she could fold into her daily teaching to planned activities that would help round out her information about him.

Engage in Kidwatching

Kidwatching (Owocki & Goodman, 2002) is a powerful tool for gaining information about students' learning and literacy development by simply standing back and observing their interactions in different environments. Teachers can kidwatch students as they transition between activities; while they play at recess; or when they are at lunch, in gym class, or in countless other places. Kidwatching involves a three-pronged focus:

1. Noting what a student knows how to do and can do
2. Determining how a student learns and conveys knowledge
3. Designing curriculum and instruction around those reflections

By paying closer attention to students' problem solving, teachers can begin to reassess their beliefs about students and build more meaningful learning contexts for them.

Set Up a Social Concerns Box

Similar to the kind of suggestion box a business might use to improve its service, teachers can set up a suggestion box for students to use to address something that concerns them. For example, this might be something that causes concern in their personal lives (e.g., "Nobody wants to sit with me at lunch"), at school (e.g., "It's not fair that you have to pay $5 to go on the fieldtrip; this means that some of us can't go"); in the local community (e.g., "I wish people would stop leaving their trash around the park"); or in a global context (e.g., "The world would be a better place for everyone if people stopped believing stereotypes about people who are different from themselves"). Teachers can ask students to think about these issues and write a suggestion once a week, maybe as part of a writing activity, or whenever they feel there's a social issue that's important to discuss—and, perhaps, to act on—as a class.

Go on a School or Community Walk: Kids "Read" Their World

Taking students on a short walk around the school or community can stimulate conversation about what concerns them that might be changed. Teachers can also supply students with cameras, asking them to snap pictures during the walk and then to write about what they've photographed (Jones, 2006). This is a quick and engaging way to learn about the issues that matter most to students. They might note that the same items sit in the "lost and found" bin week after week and that maybe some of those items can be donated to people who need them in their school or beyond. Or they might see some people asking for money or food on the streets and decide they want to inquire into why some people don't have enough money to live on their own.

WHAT TEACHERS CAN DO: TURN-AROUND STRATEGIES TO SUPPORT AND DEVELOP STUDENTS' READING FOR SOCIAL JUSTICE

Ms. Whitlow tried a few of the suggestions above to get to know Eddie better and learned that he was dealing with teasing from his classmates, who called him "girly" and "gay" because he enjoyed dancing and went to weekly dance lessons. Social injustices that students experience in their broader lives often impact classroom learning, and Eddie's solution to this problem was to pull away from others, including the friends he had made when he first moved to the school. Social injustices around issues of gender and sexuality occur every day in classrooms, schools, and all across society, and Ms. Whitlow decided that the whole class, not just Eddie, needed to read in ways that helped them notice social injustices, consider different perspectives, and be inspired to act. Fortunately, Ms. Whitlow also had several options for confronting this social issue.

Consider Texts

- Stock your classroom with texts that represent students' interests and everyday lives.
- Stock your classroom with texts that explicitly invoke discussions of social justice. An increasing number of picture books are being published that deal with issues of gender roles, homelessness, poverty, language differences, families dealing with divorce, racism, classism, incarceration, and homophobia (see the book list in the Appendix).
- Use old or currently available texts in new ways, focusing on social issues that might not be apparent on a first reading. For example, *Curious George* (Rey, 1941) can be used to talk about stealing or poaching animals, *The Giving Tree* (Silverstein, 1964) can be used for discussions about consumerism and conservation, and *Charlie and the Chocolate Factory* (Dahl, 1964) provides great material for discussions about fair trade and labor issues.
- Use text sets (books, newspaper articles, websites, photographs, video clips, etc.) that show diverse perspectives on the same topic.
- Use text resources from the Internet and other forms of media to explore social justice topics that other children have investigated across the country and the world.

Consider Teaching Structures

- Regularly provide opportunities and teach students to talk about their texts with one another in partnerships or small groups.
- Use read-aloud time to engage the whole class in discussions about texts from a social justice perspective.

- Provide more opportunities for students to investigate a social issue through their reading work, such as through inquiry approaches or units based on a particular social issue.
- Integrate reading and writing activities so students can understand that once a social issue is investigated thoroughly, they can do something about the inequities involved in it. For example, they can:

> Brainstorm resources for fieldtrip funds so that all students can go, including petitioning the board of education to spend less money on some required and costly curriculum materials so as to better support fieldtrips
>
> Create signs for the park encouraging people to throw their trash into the proper containers or inquire into whether the park has a sufficient number of trash and recycling containers accessible to people who use the park
>
> Write letters to publishing companies, asking editors to stop perpetuating stereotypes in their books and magazines

HOW THE TURN-AROUND IMPACTED EDDIE

Ms. Whitlow brought social justice issues to the forefront of her reading instruction initially by reading aloud. Eddie and his classmates were encouraged to question stereotypes about gender roles, and they began doing so by discussing what girls could do, what boys could do, and similarities and differences across genders. They found picture books, articles, and websites about girls who excelled at sports and boys who were incredible dancers. They read about female senators and male nurses, and they wrote and sent invitations to people from the community to speak with them about the professional and recreational possibilities available to both genders.

Ms. Whitlow and Eddie developed a Powerful Reading Plan (see Figure 10.1). Eddie stopped feeling ashamed about himself, and his classmates began to admire his skills. And all of Ms. Whitlow's students began reading texts with more engagement and energy, wondering what else reading could inspire them to do to make the world a better place for everyone.

FIGURE 10.1. Powerful Reading Plan

(completed by student and teacher)

Date of Plan: *February*

I, *Eddie Castillo*, plan to grow my reading practices, and over the next month I am going to focus on:

> *Looking at texts and situations from multiple perspectives.*

To reach this goal, I plan to:

1. *Find texts about the social issues that matter to me and share them with my classmates.*

2. *Keep a personal journal to record my feelings about the social issues that concern me.*

I, *Ms. Whitlow*, plan to help you grow your reading practices, and over the next month I am going to focus on:

> *Paying attention to multiple perspectives and behaviors that make some people feel excluded.*

To help you reach this goal I will:

1. *Reorganize the classroom library to help you find texts about the social issues that matter to you.*

2. *Select texts to read aloud that discuss the social issues that affect our class.*

3. *Provide opportunities for you and the class to take some social action to address the social issues that matter to us.*

Date of reflection: *March*

Student reflection on the goal(s) above: *I never thought about some of the things we're reading about now. I'm glad we're thinking about them. It makes me want to do things for other people and make the world a better place. Maybe they will do the same for me, too.*

Teacher reflection on the goal(s) above: *At first, I was nervous about teaching my students to read for social justice. I was worried that they couldn't handle it or that I wouldn't be able to explain some of the really important social issues to them because they're so young. Was I wrong about that! Take Eddie's example. Not only has he shown more engagement and enthusiasm in reading, but he's also started teaching other students about his dancing talents and everyone loves it.*

WORKING WITH ENGLISH LANGUAGE LEARNERS

- Use texts in students' native languages that explore issues of social justice, especially during read-alouds and independent reading.
- Encourage students to talk and write about their experiences as recent immigrants or children of immigrants and some of the injustices they have faced.
- Create vocabulary lists of terms and phrases, along with photographs or drawings, that are central to the issues being studied by individual students and/or the whole class.
- Connect reading, writing, and creating multimedia and digital texts by encouraging students to respond to the social injustices they are exploring through reading by alerting others to their concerns and the ways in which they're trying to change their worlds.

CONNECTIONS TO THE FIVE-PART FRAMEWORK

- *Code-breaking*: Talking about social injustices means learning to read and use new words and phrases. Through motivating units, students can learn to decode and encode words, such as *prejudice*, *discrimination*, and *homophobia*.
- *Meaning-making*: When engaged in a social action unit, students encounter many specific vocabulary words that relate to specific social and political issues. These words could be put on a word wall or added to students' vocabulary journals.
- *Text-using*: In researching a social action issue, students can use a variety of texts—such as fiction, nonfiction, editorials, and the Internet—and learn how being a text-user can support social action activities.

Who Is Struggling?
Reading Readers Differently

Some readers find themselves in situations where they are not fully participating in the practices that are deemed most important for "success" in a literacy classroom. These readers are often labeled as "struggling" and, as a consequence, receive particular kinds of attention in the classroom, outside the classroom, and in some cases in self-contained special education settings where the student population is anything but homogeneous when considering needs for literacy growth. The label "struggling reader" can harm a child in many ways, including being excluded from rich curricular engagements as a result of getting remedial reading instruction in a pull-out model and being limited to working closely with other students labeled as "struggling." These limitations erect barriers to—not opportunities for—academic achievement. Additionally, labels with negative connotations, such as "struggling reader," have psychological and social effects that can be long-standing, even lifelong. Knowing that one is considered to be struggling as a reader may cause a student to construct an identity as a nonreader, as someone who resists reading, or as someone who simply acquiesces to the fate of being a troubled reader—and often, therefore, a troubled student.

We have suggested in this book that turning around pedagogies to read readers differently may not only interrupt a trajectory of academic failure but also reengage students in interesting, meaningful, and fulfilling ways. Perhaps the millions of students identified as struggling in one way or another reflect an ongoing pedagogical struggle in the classroom, where educators don't feel prepared enough, powerful enough, or knowledgeable enough to read readers differently. When teachers read readers differently, they teach differently, talk about students differently, read books differently, and turn around their perceptions and teaching practices to respond differently. This is the most important thing teachers can do.

Reading expansively, deeply, and critically are practices that we have emphasized across this book. But this advice is not only for students in the second, third, fourth, and fifth grades, it is also for educators and everyone who supports educators. We must all engage in reading the world of classroom practice mandates and rigidity in curriculum and work to change practices that are not allowing for a more productive reading of all students. Simultaneously teachers need to read their students and work to turn themselves around to be able to influence each child in positive, powerful, critical, and joyful ways. Teachers can change the world, but the students will have to lead the way.

We began writing this book with the analogy of riding on a speeding train and suddenly realizing that the conductor has headed in the wrong direction. As a passenger, what are you to do? As we pointed out, you do have choices—not many—but you do have choices: (1) Jump off the train, (2) beg the conductor to stop, (3) find similarly angry passengers and rally together to force the conductor to stop, or (4) get off at the next stop, grab a map, and plot your next moves.

The problem with this analogy—as well as with the recent history of reading mandates, curricula, testing, and practices we have seen come down the pike—is that the passenger (or teacher) can wield very little power. There are alternatives, however, and teachers have tremendous power to wield them regarding reading practices inside their own classrooms. So now that you have taken the time to get off the train of "struggling readers," with its narrow notions of what reading is and what reading instruction should do, we recommend that you move to *rebuild the train*. This kind of reconstructed train—the train moving always toward powerful trajectories for readers in your classroom—would likely be a flexible one, one that has seats for multiple conductors and multiple tracks that allow partial and complete turn-arounds at great speed. This train might look more like a caterpillar than a freight train, and inside that train would be libraries and computers, games, drama, joyful engagement, writing, dreams, smiles, laughter, serious conversations, critical questions, and deep analysis.

We hope you will treat this book as that much-needed step off the train to reconsider the superspeed instructional strategies with which we have all been engaged at one time or another—and slow down. Students' reading trajectories can be turned around for the better, but we must be willing to turn ourselves around first.

Children's Literature

Challenging Materialism

Baylor, B. (1998). *The table where rich people sit*. New York: Aladdin Books.
Boelts, M., & Jones, N. (2007). *Those shoes*. Cambridge, MA: Candlewick Books.
McDonnel, P. (2005). *The gift of nothing*. New York: Little, Brown.
Van Allsburg, C. (1990). *Just a dream*. Boston: Houghton Mifflin.

Family Structure Diversity

Curtis, C. P. (2005). *Bud, not Buddy*. New York: Yearling.
Garza, C. L. (1990). *Family pictures/Cuadros de familia*. San Francisco: Children's Book Press.
Garza, C. L. (1996). *In my family/En mi familia*. San Francisco: Children's Book Press.
Hest, A. (1996). *Jamaica Louise James*. Cambridge, MA: Candlewick Press.
Levy, J. (1999). *Totally uncool*. Minneapolis: Carolrhoda Books.
Newman, L. (2000). *Heather has two mommies*. Los Angeles: Alyson Wonderland.
O'Connor, B. (2001). *Moonpie and Ivy*. New York: Frances Foster Books.
O'Connor, B. (2004). *Taking care of Moses*. New York: Frances Foster Books.
Parr, T. (2003). *The family book*. New York: Little, Brown Young Readers.
Rylant, C. (1996). *An angel for Solomon Singer*. New York: Scholastic.
Spinelli, E. (2000). *Night shift daddy*. New York: Hyperion.

Gender Themes

Cole, B. (1997). *Prince Cinders*. New York: Putman.
Cole, B. (2005). *Princess smartypants*. New York: Putman.
dePaola, T. (1979). *Oliver Button is a sissy*. New York: Harcourt.
Fox, M. (1994). *Tough Boris*. San Diego: Harcourt Brace.
Hoffman, A. (1991). *Amazing Grace*. New York: Dial Books.
Munsch, R. (1980). *The paper bag princess*. New York: Annick Press.
Philbrik, R. (2001). *Freak the mighty*. New York: Scholastic Signature.
Shreve, S. R. (2003). *Blister*. New York: Scholastic Signature.
Spinelli, J. (1997). *Wringer*. New York: Scholastic.
Spinelli, J. (2000). *Stargirl*. New York: Knopf.
Van Draanen, W. (1997). *How I survived being a girl*. New York: Harper-Collins.

Waber, B. (1972). *Ira sleeps over*. New York: Houghton Mifflin.

Zolotow, C. (1985). *William's doll*. New York: HarperTrophy.

Housing and Homelessness

Bunting, E. (1997). *December*. New York: Harcourt Press.

Bunting, E. (2004). *Fly away home*. Boston: Houghton Mifflin.

Disalvo, D. (2001). *A castle on Viola Street*. New York: HarperCollins.

Disalvo-Ryan, D. (1997). *Uncle Willie and the soup kitchen*. New York: HarperCollins.

Hertensten, J., & Groth, B. L. (1995). *Home is where we live: Life at a shelter through a young girl's eyes*. Chicago: Cornerstone Press.

Kaye, C. B. (2007). *A kids' guide to hunger & homelessness: How to take action! (Service Learning for Kids)*. Minneapolis: Free Spirit Publishing.

King, S. M. (2005). *Mutt dog*. New York: Harcourt.

Seskin, S., & Shamblin, A. (2006). *A chance to shine*. Berkeley: Tricycle Press.

Immigration and English Language Learning

Aliki. (1998). *Painted words/ Spoken memories: Marianthe's story*. New York: Greenwillow Books.

Anzaldua, G. (1997). *Friends from the other side/Amigos del otro lado*. San Francisco: Children's Book Press.

Atkin, S. B. (2000). *Voices from the fields: Children of migrant farmworkers tell their stories*. New York: Little, Brown.

Iijima, G. C. (2002). *The way we do it in Japan*. Morton Grove, IL: Albert Whitman & Company.

Jimenez, F., & Silva, S. (2000). *La mariposa*. San Anselmo, CA: Sandpiper Press.

Kim, J. J., & Pak, S. (2003). *Sumi's first day of school*. New York: Juvenile Press.

Levin, E. (1989). *I hate English!* New York: Scholastic.

Surat, M. (1983). *Angel child, dragon child*. Milwaukee: Raintree Publishers.

Incarcerated Parent Themes

Williams, V. B. (2004). *Amber was brave, Essie was smart*. New York: HarperTrophy.

Woodson, J. (2002). *Visiting day*. New York: Scholastic.

Kids and Communities Working for Social Change

Cole, K. (2001). *No bad news*. Morton Grove, IL: Albert Whitman & Company.

Disalvo-Ryan, D. (1994). *City green*. New York: HarperCollins.

Joseph, L. (2001). *The color of my words*. New York: HarperCollins.

Kurusa, M. D., & Englander, K. (1995). *The streets are free*. Toronto, Canada: Annick Press.

Wyeth, S. D. (1998). *Something beautiful*. New York: Dragonfly Books.

Multiple Perspectives

Euwer Wolff, V. (2000). *Bat 6*. New York: Scholastic.

Fleishman, P. (1997). *Seedfolks*. New York: HarperTrophy.

Hall, D. (1994). *I am the dog, I am the cat*. New York: Dial.

Hesse, K. (2001). *Witness*. New York: Scholastic.

Hoberman, M. A. (2001). *You read to me, I'll read to you: Very short fairy tales to read together*. New York: Little, Brown.

Macaulay, D. (1990). *Black and white*. Boston: Houghton Mifflin.

Schanzer. R. (2004). *George vs. George: The American Revolution as seen from both sides*. Washington, DC: National Geographic.

Van Draanen, W. (2001). *Flipped*. New York: Knopf.

Yolen, J. (1992). *Encounter*. New York: Voyager Books.

Young, E. (1993). *Seven blind mice*. New York: Scholastic.

"Paying It Forward": Working for Others' Benefit

Carmi, G. (2003). *A circle of friends*. Long Island City, NY: Star Bright Books.

Hillenbrand, J., & Hillenbrand, W. (2006). *What a treasure*. New York: Holiday House.

Race and Ethnic Diversity

Adoff, A. (2002). *Black is brown is tan*. New York: HarperCollins.

Choi, Y. (2003). *The name jar*. New York: Dragonfly Books.

Cisneros, S. (1991). *The house on Mango Street*. New York: Vintage.

Flake, S. (2007). *The skin I'm in*. New York: Hyperion Books.

Fox, M. (2006). *Whoever you are*. New York: Voyager Books.

hooks, b. (2004). *Skin again*. New York: Hyperion Books.

Katz, K. (1999). *The colors of us*. New York: Henry Holt and Company.

Keats, E. J. (2003). *My name is Yoon*. New York: Farrar, Straus & Giroux.

Kissinger, K. (2002). *All the colors we are: Todos los colores de nuestra piel/ The story of how we get our skin color*. Pittsburgh, PA: Redlead Press.

Rylant, C. (1998). *Appalachia: The voices of sleeping birds*. San Anselmo, CA: Sandpiper.

Soto, G. (2000). *Baseball in April and other stories*. New York: Harcourt Paperbacks.

Tyler, M. (2005). *The skin you live in*. Chicago: Chicago Children's Museum.

Woodson, J. (2003). *The house you pass on the way*. New York: Puffin.

Social Class Diversity and Economic Struggle

Atkins, J. (1998). *Get set! Swim!* New York: Lee & Low Books.

Browne, A. (2001). *Voices in the park*. New York: DK Children.

Cooper, M., & Bennett, N. (2000). *Gettin' through Thursday*. New York: Lee & Low Books.

Hazen, B. S. (1984). *Tight times*. New York: Puffin.

Jackson, I. (1996). *Somebody's new pajamas*. New York: Dial Books for Young Readers.

O'Connor, B. (2008). *Fame and glory in Freedom, Georgia*. New York: Frances Foster Books.

O'Connor, B. (2009). *How to steal a dog*. New York: SquareFish.

Perez, A. I., & Gonzalez, M. C. (2008). *My very own room/Mi propio curatito*. San Francisco: Children's Book Press.

Spinelli, J. (2008). *Eggs*. New York: Little, Brown.

Steig, W. (1988). *Brave Irene*. New York: Farrar, Straus & Giroux.

Williams, V. B. (1984). *A chair for my mother*. New York: HarperTrophy.

Williams, V. B. (1986). *Something special for me*. New York: HarperTrophy.

Vocabulary and Word Work

Banks, K. (2006). *Max's words*. New York: Farrar, Straus & Giroux.

Clements, A. (1997). *Double trouble in Walla Walla*. Minneapolis: Carolrhoda Books.

DeGross, M. (1994). *Donavan's word jar*. New York: HarperTrophy.

Falwell, C. (1998). *Word wizard*. New York: Clarion.

Frasier, D. (2000). *Miss Alanineus: A vocabulary disaster*. New York: Harcourt.

Schotter, R. (2006). *The boy who loved words*. New York: Schwarz & Wade Books.

Shulman, M. (2006). *Mom and dad are palindromes*. San Francisco: Chronicle Books.

Turner, P. (1996). *The war between the vowels and the consonants*. New York: Farrar, Straus & Giroux.

Walton, R. (1997). *Pig, pigger, piggest*. Salt Lake City, UT: Gibbs Smith.

Walton, R. (1998). *Why the banana split*. Salt Lake City, UT: Gibbs Smith.

Work, Workers, and Labor Issues

Borden, L. (1990). *The neighborhood trucker*. New York: Scholastic.

Bunting, E. (1994). *A day's work*. New York: Clarion.

Bunting, E., & Payne, C. F. (2006). *Pop's bridge*. New York: Harcourt Children's Books.

Cohn, D. (2002). *Si se puede! Yes we can! Janitor strike in L.A.* El Paso, TX: Cinco Puntos Press.

Hartland, J. (2007). *Night shift*. New York: Bloomsbury Children's Books.

Isaacs, G. L. (1991). *While you are asleep . . .* New York: Walker & Company.

London, J. (1996). *The village basket weaver*. New York: Dutton Children's Books.

References

Aliki. (1998). *Marianthe's story: Painted words and spoken memories*. New York: HarperCollins.

Allington, R. L. (2005). *What really matters for struggling readers: Designing research-based programs* (2nd ed.). New York: Longman.

Armbruster, B., Lehr, F., & Osborn, J. (2001). *Put reading first*. Washington, DC: National Institute for Literacy.

Bear, D. R., Invernizzi, M., Templeton, S., & Johnston, F. (2008). *Words their way: Word study for phonics, vocabulary, and spelling instruction*. Upper Saddle River, NJ: Pearson.

Bunting, E. (1994). *A day's work*. New York: Clarion.

Calkins, L. M. (2001). *The art of teaching reading*. New York: Longman.

Cleary, B. (1953). *Otis Spofford*. New York: HarperCollins.

Comber, B., & Kamler, B. (Eds.). (2005). *Turn-around pedagogies: Literacy interventions for at-risk students*. Newton, Australia: Primary English Teaching Association.

Coiro, J. (2003). Reading comprehension on the Internet: Expanding our understanding of reading comprehension to encompass new literacies. *The Reading Teacher, 56*, 458–464.

Coiro, J., & Dobler, E. (2007). Exploring the online reading comprehension strategies used by sixth-grade skilled readers to search for and locate information on the Internet. *Reading Research Quarterly, 42*, 214–257.

Craighead George, J. (1959). *My side of the mountain*. New York: Penguin.

Dahl, R. (1964). *Charlie and the chocolate factory*. New York: Penguin Putnam.

Davis, F. B. (1944). Fundamental factors of comprehension in reading. *Psychometrika, 9*, 185–197.

Disalvo-Ryan, D. (1997). *Uncle Willie and the soup kitchen*. New York: HarperCollins.

Dreher, M. J. (2003). Motivating struggling readers by tapping the potential of information books. *Reading and Writing Quarterly, 19*(1), 25–38.

Duke, N. K. (2004). The case for informational text. *Educational Leadership, 61*(6), 40–44.

Fitzgerald, J., & Graves, M. F. (2004). *Scaffolding reading experiences for English-language learners*. Norwood, MA: Christopher-Gordon.

Fleishman, P. (1997). *Seedfolks*. New York: HarperTrophy.

Freebody, P., & Luke, A. (1990). Literacies programs: Debates and demands in cultural context. *Prospect: Australian Journal of TESOL, 5*(7), 7–16.

Freire, P. (1970). *Pedagogy of the oppressed.* New York: Continuum.

Graves, M. F. (2006). *The vocabulary book: Learning and instruction.* New York: Teachers College Press.

Graves, M. F. (2008). *Teaching individual words: One size does not fit all.* New York: Teachers College Press.

Harris, A. J., & Sipay, E. R. (1990). *How to increase reading ability* (8th ed.). New York: Longman.

Hart, B., & Risley, T. R. (2003, Spring). The early catastrophe: The 30 million word gap. *American Educator, 27,* 4–9.

Harvey, S., & Goudvis, A. (2007). *Strategies that work: Teaching comprehension for understanding and engagement.* Portland, ME: Stenhouse.

Jones, S. (2006). *Girls, social class and literacy: What teachers can do to make a difference.* Portsmouth, NH: Heinemann.

Jones, S., & Clarke, L. W. (2007). Disconnect: Pushing readers beyond connections and toward the critical. *Pedagogies, 2*(2), 95–115.

Kamler, B., & Comber, B. (2005). Turn-around pedagogies: Improving the education of at-risk students. *Improving Schools, 8*(2), 121–131.

Keene, E. O., & Zimmerman, S. (2007). *Mosaic of thought: The power of comprehension strategy instruction.* Portsmouth, NH: Heinemann.

Labbo, L. D., Eakle, A. J., & Montero, M. K. (2002, May). Digital language experience approach: Using digital photographs and software as a language experience approach innovation. *Reading Online, 5*(8). Retrieved June 2, 2009, from: http://www.readingonline.org/electronic/elec_index.asp?HREF=labbo2/index.html

Luke, A., & Freebody, P. (1999). A map of possible practices: Further notes on the four resources model. *Practically Primary, 4*(2), 5–8.

Meyer, B. J. F. (1985). Prose analysis: Purposes, procedures, and problems. In B. K. Britton & J. B. Black (Eds.), *Understanding expository text* (pp. 11–64). Hillsdale, NJ: Erlbaum.

Minarik, E. H. (1978). *Little bear.* New York: HarperTrophy.

Moss, B. (2004a). Fabulous, fascinating fact books. *Instructor, 113*(8), 28–29, 65.

Moss, B. (2004b). Teaching expository text structures through information trade book retellings. *The Reading Teacher, 57*(8), 710–718.

Owocki, G., & Goodman, Y. (2002). *Kidwatching: Documenting children's literacy development.* Portsmouth, NH: Heinemann.

Pressley, M., Rankin, J., & Yokoi, L. (1996). A survey of instructional practices of primary teachers nominated as effective in promoting literacy. *The Elementary School Journal, 96*(4), 363–384.

Rasinski, T., & Padak, N. (2000). *Effective reading strategies: Teaching children who find reading difficult* (2nd ed.). Columbus, OH: Merrill/Prentice Hall.

Rey, H. A. (1941). *Curious George.* Boston: Houghton Mifflin.

Roessel, D., & Rampersad, A. (Eds.). (2006). *Poetry for young people: Langston Hughes.* New York: Scholastic.

Rush, L. S. (2004). First steps toward a full and flexible literacy: Case studies of the four resources model. *Reading Research and Instruction, 43*(3), 37–55.

Rylant, C. (1997). *Henry and Mudge and the best day of all.* New York: Scholastic.

Schanzer, R. (2004). *George vs. George: The American Revolution as seen from both sides.* Washington, DC: National Geographic.

Siegel, M., Kontovourki, S., Schmier, S., & Enriquez, G. (2008). Literacy in motion: A case study of a shape-shifting kindergartner. *Language Arts, 86,* 89–98.

Silverstein, S. (1964). *The giving tree.* New York: HarperCollins.

Spector, K. (2009). Manoeurveings: Either side of the violet tint. In J. Van Galen & V. Dempsey (Eds.), *Trajectories: The social and educational mobility of education scholars from poor and working class backgrounds* (pp. 95–106). Rotterdam, The Netherlands: Sense Publishers.

Spencer, B. H. (2003). Text maps: Helping students navigate informational texts. *The Reading Teacher, 56*(8), 752–756.

Strickland, D. (1998). *Teaching phonics today: A primer for educators.* Newark, DE: International Reading Association.

Taberski, S. (2000). *On solid ground: Strategies for teaching reading K–3.* Portsmouth, NH: Heinemann.

Watts-Taffe, S., & Gwinn, C. B. (2007). *Integrating literacy and technology: Effective practice for grades K–6.* New York: Guilford.

Williams, V. B. (2001). *Amber was brave, Essie was smart.* New York: HarperCollins.

Wilson, J. L., & Laman, T. T. (2007). "That was basically me": Critical literacy, text, and talk. *Voices from the Middle, 15*(2), 40–46.

Wylie, R., & Durrell, D. (1970). Teaching vowels through phonograms. *Elementary English, 47,* 787–791.

Yolen, J. (1992). *Encounter.* New York: Voyager Books.

Index

About the Authors

Stephanie Jones is an associate professor of education at the University of Georgia. A former classroom teacher and professional developer, Stephanie is the author of *Girls, Social Class, and Literacy: What Teachers Can Do to Make a Difference* and numerous book chapters and articles in journals such as *Anthropology and Education Quarterly, Changing English, Feminist Teacher, Journal of Adolescent and Adult Literacy, Language Arts, Pedagogies, Reading Research Quarterly, The Reading Teacher,* and others. Stephanie's interests include critical literacy; identity; gender and social class; education for social justice; place-based pedagogies; and working with classroom teachers, principals, children, and families to make schools a safer and more productive place for everyone.

Lane W. Clarke is an assistant professor in literacy at Northern Kentucky University. A former classroom teacher and reading intervention specialist, Lane received her Ed.D. from the University of Cincinnati. Lane has published numerous articles about literacy in journals such as *Language Arts, English Journal, Journal of Literacy Research, The Reading Teacher,* and *The Journal of Adolescent and Adult Literacy.* She has also written book chapters and has an edited book coming out with Prufrock Press about integrating technology in the content areas. Her interests include reading comprehension, using literature circles in the classroom, working with readers facing challenges in traditional classrooms, and using instructional technology in the literacy classroom.

Grace Enriquez is an assistant professor in language and literacy at Lesley University. She received her doctorate from Teachers College, Columbia University, and is an American Association of University Women fellowship recipient. A former staff developer and a language arts and reading classroom teacher, she has worked with students and teachers throughout New Jersey, New England, Philadelphia, and New York City. Grace has presented at national conferences and published articles in *Language Arts, Reading Research Quarterly, The ALAN Review,* and *The Journal of Children's Literature.* Her research interests include literacy and identity, critical literacy, literacy and technology, and urban education.